AIRBORNE

Hero: The Buzz Beurling Story

King's War: Mackenzie King and the Politics of War
1939–1945

Champagne Navy: Canada's Small Boat Raiders
of the Second World War
(with Brian Jeffrey Street)

AIRBORNE

The Heroic Story of the 1st Canadian Parachute Battalion in the Second World War

Brian Nolan

Canadian Cataloguing in Publication Data

Nolan, Brian
    Airborne: the heroic story of the 1st Canadian Parachute Battalion
in the Second World War

Includes bibliographical references and index.
ISBN 1-895555-77-9

1. Canada. Canadian Army. Canadian Parachute Battalion, 1st — History.
2. World War, 1939-1945 — Regimental histories — Canada. I. Title.

UA602.C2942N6   1995   940.54'1271   C95-931363-X

Lester Publishing Limited
56 The Esplanade
Toronto, Ontario
Canada M5E 1A7

Printed and bound in Canada

95 96 97 98 5 4 3 2 1

To Anne Acland

All these were honoured in their generations,
and were the glory of their times.

Ecclesiasticus 44:7

CONTENTS

AUTHOR'S NOTE

SEPTEMBER 25, 1993. CAMP PETAWAWA, ONTARIO, HOME OF THE Canadian Airborne Regiment. The day dawned in brilliant sunshine. The first maples were aflame with colour. At precisely 2:00 P.M., Canada's elite band of paratroopers marched onto the base's parade square for the trooping of the colour to mark the twenty-fifth anniversary of the regiment's beginnings. It was planned to be a day of celebration. Yet, when the more than six hundred men stepped smartly into Nicklin Square in their distinctive maroon berets, crisply pressed khaki summer uniforms, and gleaming "jump" boots, they marched under a cloud of suspicion. For months, newspaper and television newscasts were filled with disturbing reports of wrongdoing by some members of the regiment while serving as peacekeepers in the lawless wastes of Somalia. By the end of March 1994, with the last of seven courts martial, Canadians came to know the awful truth of how a sixteen-year-old boy was tortured to death, and another victim shot to death in the back; of a concentrated effort at the top of the military high command to cover up criminal activity; and of Canadian paratroopers vowing "to kill niggers."

In the wake of the testimony there came to light the existence of two home-made videotapes, one documenting bizarre initiation rituals, and the other containing racial slurs. The combination of the videos and the earlier courts martial testimony resulted in a swift and stunning decision to disband the

ix

controversial regiment, the first time in Canadian military history that a unit was so disgraced.

What went wrong? The question, Canadians hope, will be answered in the findings of a blue-chip panel of prominent civilians who are expected to table their report by the end of 1995, following coast-to-coast public hearings.

When I first began the research for this book in the summer of 1992, the scandal surrounding the Canadian Airborne Regiment had yet to unfold. In fact, the regiment hadn't even left Canada for peacekeeping duties in Somalia, and wouldn't do so until December 1992. Airborne was hardly a household word either, back then. When I told friends and colleagues what I was working on, most thought the airborne was something to do with the air force. I discovered many Canadians couldn't identify the regiment's famous maroon beret. All that changed after March 16, 1993, the night the sixteen-year-old Somalian suspected thief was captured sneaking around the Canadian paratroopers' camp outside Belet Huen, Somalia.

The Canadian Airborne Regiment was really the son of two Canadian paratroop battalions: the 2nd Canadian Parachute Battalion, which was part of the First Special Service Force, commonly known as the Devil's Brigade; and the 1st Canadian Parachute Battalion, which is the object of my research.

As the research material piled up, it became clear just how different the wartime paratroop battalions were from the now disbanded Canadian Airborne Regiment. They were, as was the Canadian Army in the Second World War, made up of civilians, and not professional soldiers like the present Canadian Army and its active regiments. Indeed, it is worth reminding ourselves that, of the five fighting divisions during the war, three were led by non-professionals. Even more revealing was how few permanent force soldiers, "PFs," as they were known, made up the 1st Canadian Parachute

Battalion — perhaps three at most. Another fact worth recounting is that the active Canadian Army of 1939–45 was better trained than any of the country's professional peacetime soldiers at that time, a remarkable achievement that is lost in time and in the current military rhetoric of how important it is to have a standing professional army.

The 1st Canadian Parachute Battalion was unique in another way. Many of Canada's great fighting regiments were drawn from local militia units whose soldiers came from perhaps one large city, the Royal Hamilton Light Infantry, the famous "Rileys," is a good example, or from small-town units, which attracted members from the surrounding countryside, such as the "Hasty Pees," the Hastings and Prince Edward Regiment, of eastern Ontario. Instead, Canada's premier paratroop battalion was made up of Canadians from every part of the land, Quebec included, a mixture of boys from farm and city who served with distinction. When peace was finally won, Canada's first paratroopers dispersed as quickly as they had answered the call to arms. No one has captured in words the spirit of their contribution or the meaning of their sacrifice as well as military historian Colonel C. P. Stacey in his salute to *all* of Canada's sons and daughters who served in this army of the just.

> They left a trail of triumphs behind them, and did honour to their country wherever they set the print of their hobnailed boots. The Army that did these things is already little more than a memory. Many thousands of those who made its reputation sleep in alien ground; and of the survivors the vast majority have returned to civilian pursuits and are scattered about the country and the world. Canadians will do well, however, to cherish the recollection of this remarkable fighting force. In the most desperate crisis of which human records tell, it was

Canada's strong right arm. With it she intervened on the world's battlefield and struck good blows for the good cause. The men and women who made up this army dispersed gladly about their business when their task was done. They left to their fellow-Canadians, for today, the peace which they and their brave comrades of other services and other lands had bought with toil and blood; for tomorrow, and the myriad perils and uncertainties with which tomorrow is always fraught, they bequeathed to their countrymen, for their inspiration and support, a tradition of service, sacrifice and victory.

The members of the 1st Canadian Parachute Battalion themselves bequeathed to the paratroopers who followed them a special legacy to hold, guard, and honour — their battle colours. With the disbandment of the Canadian Airborne Regiment, these colours have been retired.

It seems to me the time was never more appropriate to remember the contribution of Canada's first paratroop soldiers before their record fades from memory, or is left awash in the wake of the controversial disbandment of the Canadian Airborne Regiment, a decision that has created conflicting emotions throughout the land. This is the true story of the 1st Canadian Parachute Battalion and the honours it won on the battlefields of Europe during the Second World War.

Brian Nolan
Sanxay, France
Spring 1995

1

THE LOST BATTALION

He . . . never had a chance.

Ben Malkin, war correspondent for the Winnipeg Free Press, *reporting*
the death of Lieutenant-Colonel Jeff Nicklin, commanding officer of the
1st Canadian Parachute Battalion in Germany, March 1945

PARATROOPERS ARE ELUSIVE COMBATANTS. TRYING TO FIND one after he has jumped into battle is like knowing where the circus went the morning after it packed up the tents and slipped out of town. Yet that was the assignment handed to a Canadian Army rear-echelon captain named R. A. Virtue and his driver, Ted Gold, on the last day of March 1945. Virtue was charged with finding not only one paratrooper, but an entire battalion of them.

Canada's most celebrated paratrooper, Jeff Nicklin, former

Winnipeg Blue Bomber football star, had just led the 1st Canadian Parachute Battalion in the second-biggest airborne operation of the Second World War — a stupendous parachute assault on the soil of the Third Reich east of the Rhine River. The day before Virtue set out, Defence Headquarters in Ottawa had reported that Nicklin was missing in action. The news shocked Winnipegers, and left many Canadian football fans inconsolable. Nicklin was a brilliant athlete, a man idolized on and off the gridiron. Questions were raised in the House of Commons. Was Nicklin missing or not? Was he dead? Ottawa demanded answers from Canadian Military Headquarters in London and the headquarters of the 21 Army Group on the European continent. Clouding the issue was a signal from the Second British Army on March 29 that emphatically said: "Lt.-Col. Nicklin reported missing 24 March '45 NOT killed."

To describe the 1st Canadian Parachute Battalion as a "lost" battalion is not to exaggerate. As part of the 6th British Airborne Division, the battalion often got lost in the small print of accounts detailing the triumphs of this famous British airborne division, long a sore point with many veterans of the battalion and members of the 1st Canadian Parachute Battalion Association. Ronald F. "Andy" Anderson, longtime president of the association, said, "I've always thought we were the lost battalion. Under British command we were out of sight and out of mind to Canadians back home." Anderson regrettably learned during preparations for the fiftieth anniversary of D-Day that present-day journalists were equally ignorant of the battalion's tragedies and triumphs. "They didn't even know that Canadian paratroopers were a part of D-Day," Anderson said.

In fact, many Canadian paratroopers were among the first Allied troops to land on French soil, hours before the assault troops splashed ashore on the beaches. Of the three biggest Allied airborne operations of the Second World War, D-Day, Arnhem, and the Rhine crossing, Canadians were in the forefront of two — D-Day and the Rhine drop. Moreover, the 1st Canadian Parachute Battalion was the only Canadian unit to fight in the Ardennes, where Hitler launched his last desperate counter-attack through the snowy forests of Belgium in hopes of reaching the vital Allied port of Antwerp. By war's end, the 1st Canadian Parachute Battalion had advanced farther into the heart of Germany than any other Canadian fighting men, not stopping until it reached the shores of the Baltic Sea in a breathtaking campaign about which little has been written.

Aside from adapting and refining the newest art of war, the 1st Canadian Parachute Battalion was the most uniquely Canadian army formation of the Second World War. While the majority of wartime regiments were formed from home-grown militia units of the non-permanent force, the parachute battalion was made up of volunteers from every province and territory of Canada. The volunteers came from all walks of life — they were doctors, lawyers, priests, ministers, teachers, labourers, mechanics, machinists, university students, mill hands, milkmen, bakers, and farmers — and from various ethnic backgrounds — English, French, Scottish, Irish, Ukrainian, Polish, Russian, Finnish, Norwegian, and Swedish, to name a few. There was also a large representation of native peoples from various tribes. Surprisingly, the unit attracted dozens of Americans, who crossed the border to volunteer. Few units in the Canadian Army could boast of such an eclectic mix in its ranks. The variety produced a good-natured comradeship where invariably anyone from Quebec became "Frenchy," anyone west of the Ontario border, "Cowboy," and native Canadians, "Chief."

What really made the battalion stand apart, however, was its proud record of never failing to take an objective assigned to it and, once taken, never losing it.

It is doubtful that when Captain Virtue set out to find the battalion he was even vaguely aware of the Canadian paratroopers' short, enviable record. We don't know much about Virtue except that he seems an irrepressible character from the account he left us of his search for the battalion and the fate of its commanding officer.

After crossing the Rhine, Virtue sped eastward and the towns he passed through — Wesel, Peddenberg, Haltern, Coesfeld, Billerbeck, Münster, and Greven — must have given him some clue how rapidly the Canadians were moving. His report reads like a German railway timetable. What Virtue found in the wake of the battalion's advance were scenes nothing short of Armageddon. Everywhere there were dead German soldiers "in the main streets and in the pastures adjoining the highway," Virtue reported. "Horses and cattle of all descriptions had not escaped the blast of air and artillery bombardment and carcasses lay everywhere with everyone too busy to do anything about disposal."

Virtue's acute observations provide one of the few accounts by an outsider who reported on any of the unit's campaigns. The breadth of destruction left in the wake of the Canadians' advance is sobering: flattened buildings, bridges blown up, blackened and charred gun pits, and everywhere the sweet, sickly smell of death, so pervasive no one could escape its presence. The first wildflowers of spring only added a surrealistic patina to this horrifying landscape.

Along the way Virtue and Gold were shot at by snipers and shelled by mortars whose shrapnel rattled the hood of the jeep. In addition, Virtue was convinced he was the object of several V-2 rocket attacks. Whenever he asked the whereabouts of the 1st Canadian Parachute Battalion, he was told "they went that way." He had started out at noon on March 31, 1945, and finally, by nine o'clock that night, he came upon the Canadian paratroopers near Greven and the Dortmund-Ems Canal.

Virtue discovered soon enough what had happened to Lieutenant-Colonel Nicklin. He had never reached the ground the day the Canadians jumped into Germany. That was shortly after ten o'clock on the morning of March 24, seven days previously. Landing in a copse of trees in the middle of the drop zone, Nicklin's body was riddled with machine-gun bullets from a nearby German gun pit. As Ben Malkin, the *Winnipeg Free Press* war correspondent, wrote: "He never landed, never got rid of his 'chute, never fought, and never had a chance."

The news was reported to Virtue by Nicklin's fiery successor, Major Fraser Eadie, who had taken command of the battalion after Nicklin's death. When Virtue reached Eadie, the battalion was under sniper fire and was about to mount an assault on the Dortmund-Ems Canal, three hundred yards distant. Virtue's account of meeting Eadie surely will bring smiles to the faces of all those paratroopers who served under the feisty commanding officer. "Briefly, the CO was not impressed," Virtue wrote of their meeting, "and after expressing himself freely (and who could blame him; it was not a timely interruption) he offered all the information required."

The confirmation of Jeff Nicklin's death left Winnipegers disconsolate with grief, no one more so than Nicklin's young widow, Eileen. The athlete's son, David Jeff, whom Nicklin had never seen, was too young to comprehend the tragedy.

While Virtue turned his jeep around and headed westwards, the 1st Canadian Parachute Battalion advanced through the suburbs of Greven. They were about to begin a brilliant dash across Germany that covered three hundred miles in six weeks. In retrospect, it was a stunning campaign that was a near textbook example of airborne operations, from the frenzied jump just east of the Rhine to the deadly and recurring series of assaults against an enemy implacable to the end. The Canadians demonstrated that they had learned the tenets of airborne fighting, and had perfected them in three remarkable years of warring in sunshine and in shadow.

2
AN INFINITE DEAL
OF MISCHIEF

Five thousand balloons capable of raising two men
each could not cost more than five ships of the line; and
where is the prince who can afford so to cover his country
with troops for its defense as that ten thousand men
descending from the clouds might not in many places
do an infinite deal of mischief before a force could
be brought together to repel them.

Benjamin Franklin, 1784

IN 1936, MILITARY OBSERVERS WHO WATCHED THE RUSSIANS parachute two battalions with 16 light field guns and 150 machine-guns onto a field outside of Kiev were awakened to the potential of what they had just witnessed. For centuries practitioners of the art of war dreamt, designed, and launched any number of manoeuvres to outflank their enemies. Now, by arranging one swoop from the sky, a general could place an attacking force anywhere he desired, adhering to Napoleon's maxim: if you can outflank the enemy, you will surely derange and confuse him.

The Soviets demonstrated in a dramatic way how to capitalize on the use of air transport to take men into battle. The Kiev drop perhaps didn't rank with the invention of either the machine-gun or the tank, but it added a new dimension to the face of war. If that was not proof enough of future paratroopers' potential, the Russians followed this display with another demonstration, near Moscow, in September 1936, when they dropped 5,200 paratroopers in a single jump. Again, military observers were filled with anticipation of what the future of airborne warfare held for those bold enough to grasp and develop the concept. A year earlier, the Red Army had transported an entire division in a fleet of transport planes from Moscow to Vladivostok, employing a tactic that became known as "airlanding."

These three manoeuvres — the two mass parachute drops and the airlift of an entire division — combined with German efforts in the early 1930s to pull two hundred armed troops in a giant glider across the sky, constituted the three major components of airborne warfare: parachute assault, glider attack, and airlanding by transport planes of well-equipped troops ready to fight. The Russians made a documentary film to show the world the possible future of airborne operations, but it was the Germans who first applied theory to practice.

In early May 1940, Hitler was ready to move into The Netherlands, Belgium, and France. On May 10, German paratroopers, in a lightning-swift series of drops, captured all the bridges key to the defence of Rotterdam and The Hague in The Netherlands. On the same day, in an even more spectacular assault, other German glider troops struck in Belgium. The Belgians planned their defence of the country along the Meuse River between Namur and Liège and the Albert Canal from Liège to Antwerp. Along this line was a series of so-called impregnable fortresses, the main one being Fort Eben Emael, defended by one thousand troops. Ten gliders carrying just seventy-eight German troops landed literally on top of the fortress's earthen works and the soldiers set to work destroying its turrets and casements. Three hundred additional German paratroopers jumped shortly after the gliders touched down to support the initial attack. By noon the next day Fort Eben Emael surrendered. The German paras also took three key bridges, two over the Albert Canal and one over the Meuse River. With these bridges intact, German mechanized and armoured columns rumbled forward, flattening whatever resistance was left.

The Germans mounted their next airborne assault in Greece in April 1941, when nearly two thousand paras descended on the only bridge across the Corinth Canal, hoping to trap a British brigade. They almost did, but had not reckoned on a daring evacuation by the Royal Navy, who got most of the brigade out of the Peloponnese.

Ten days later, on May 20, the German paras were in the air again for the biggest airborne attack the Germans ever attempted: the air assault on the island of Crete, the largest island in the Aegean Sea. The Luftwaffe hoped to use Crete as a base from which to attack British convoys in the eastern Mediterranean and to offer air support for Erwin Rommel's Afrika Korps, who were fighting in Libya with designs to capture Cairo.

The Germans gambled that Crete was soon to be theirs. Under command of Colonel-General Kurt Student, who would come to haunt British paratroopers in a future airborne operation in Holland, the Germans led fifteen thousand airborne troops in a massive assault by parachute, gliders, and airlanding by transport planes. While it was indeed the largest airborne operation ever mounted by Germany, it turned out to be the most disastrous. Although the island was captured after fierce and often hand-to-hand fighting, the number of German casualties was incredibly high. One of every four paras was killed. The total losses for Operation Merkur (Mercury) were over 30 per cent. Student called it "the grave of the German paratroopers." The German victory at Crete was "at once the zenith and the nadir of the German airborne," said Charles B. MacDonald, former deputy chief historian of the U.S. Army.

Hitler, incensed at the huge loss of life, decided in his own mind that airborne warfare was too costly. He never again approved any large-scale operations involving German paratroopers, although small groups were used daringly on two occasions. The first, a German glider force, landed in northern Italy to rescue Italian dictator Benito Mussolini, who was being held under arrest by the Italian government after it joined the Allied side. The second operation was less successful. German paratroopers and glider troops dropped on another mountain top, this one in Yugoslavia in 1944, hoping to capture Josip Tito in his mountain hideaway, but the crafty partisan eluded them. Several operations were planned for the Russian front but were never carried out. A battalion of German paras was dropped in the Battle of the Ardennes just before Christmas 1944, but the troops were so widely scattered they offered no threat. Hitler remained adamant, however, that there would be no airborne operations the size of Crete. German paratroopers would fight as infantry.

"Few of Hitler's decisions were more fateful for the conduct of the war," wrote Edwin P. Hoyt, author of *Airborne: The History of American Parachute Forces*. "In the final days, when Fortress Europe was besieged, German airborne troops might have created havoc among the advancing armies. Luckily, after Crete, the initiative in airborne operations moved to the western Allies." Hitler's decision remains a strange one, especially in light of his record of committing tens of thousands of young German soldiers to fight to the death in Russia, where the odds of surviving either the Russian winter or the Red Army were indeed long.

The disastrous results of Crete did not negatively influence Allied war planners' views of the effectiveness of airborne operations. In fact, the exact opposite was true. If Crete had been a failure for the Germans, the capture of Fort Eben Emael by them and the parallel parachute attack in The Netherlands had convinced the British and the Americans that parachute warfare was viable, even though both nations were far behind the Soviet Union and Germany in developing airborne units of any effective size. Winston Churchill recognized early on the tactical value of raising airborne divisions. On June 22, 1940, he strongly suggested to the War Cabinet, "We ought to have a corps of at least five thousand parachute troops."

In quick order the wheels were set in motion for developing a contingent of British paratroopers. The Air Ministry established a parachute training centre at Ringway, the civilian airport just outside of Manchester in England's industrial north. The Royal Air Force (RAF) instructors would teach parachute jumping, and the RAF transport pilots would fly the troopers into battle. By late 1940 the first of the thousands and thousands of gliders turned out during the war were put on order. So little credence had been given to airborne operations that there was not much information available on how troops should be trained for this new arm of the British army. Pathetically, the old Russian documentary film, which included sequences of the Kiev jumps, was dusted off in hopes the scenes would give planners some clue as to how to develop a force of paratroopers.

The situation was no different in the United States. It was not until June 1940 that the army brass in Washington gave the go-ahead to form a test platoon, which grew to battalion size by the autumn of 1940. After the War Department studied the details of the fall of Crete in 1941, it ordered the formation of three more battalions, which, by the end of the year, was successfully achieved.

Throughout all these developments, Canada was a watchful spectator. One exception was Colonel E. L. M. Burns, who was an original thinker. As a captain back in 1924 with the Royal Canadian Engineers, Burns had written an article proposing the mechanization of cavalry. Condemning the horse as obsolete and inefficient, Burns went on to propose that cavalry units be put aboard motorized vehicles capable of moving a machine-gun across country at fifteen miles an hour. This was considered heresy. As late as 1936 there were those in the Canadian Army who argued that mounted cavalry could outmanoeuvre tanks any day.

In August 1940, Burns, now a colonel, suggested an equally radical idea. He proposed to a fellow colonel, J. C. Murchie, that Canada raise a unit of paratroopers. Murchie didn't like the idea for a number of reasons. Most important, he felt such an outfit needed its own special infrastructure to train and deliver the troops into battle. Murchie concluded that to form an exclusively Canadian airborne unit was not practical and, if one was formed, it most surely would have to be attached to a British airborne unit and, hence, would not be under Canadian control. In this war, unlike the First World War, Canada wanted to be autonomous. Murchie turned down the proposal, but Burns wouldn't take no for an answer.

A few weeks later, Burns went directly to the chief general staff, urging them to think the proposal through. He wasn't asking for an offensive airborne unit but rather a defensive one, raising the issue of possible invasion on Canada's west coast, where airborne troops could be quickly rushed in to counter-attack the invaders. Headquarters dumped cold water on this idea as well. Undaunted, Burns kept at the brass, but to no avail.

It was not until June 1942 that National Defence Head-quarters had a change of heart, convinced, it seems, by the American initiative. Headquarters dispatched Lieutenant-Colonel R. H. Keefler to Fort Benning, Georgia, to study U.S. training methods, logistics, and airborne techniques, all of which would be considered as a basic plan for training a Canadian parachute battalion. Camp Shilo in Manitoba was selected as the airborne training centre but, as it turned out, Shilo was not immediately available. Until it was, an agreement was worked out between Washington and Ottawa to train the Canadians in Georgia, and that's where the first volunteers headed in the middle of August 1942.

Paratroopers are by nature a demonstrative lot. If jumping out of an airplane is not a theatrical act, then nothing is. As the army discovered early, there were certain traits that made a good jumper. Ironically, some of the attributes the army wanted in a paratrooper were diametrically opposite to those they looked for in an infantryman, artillery gunner, or tank crewman. What set the paratrooper apart from his fellow soldiers was his ability to think on his own and be decisive in his actions. The possibility of being separated from his comrades in battle was a real one, as the 1st Canadian Parachute Battalion discovered when it dropped through the night sky on D-Day in its first combat jump. It was crucial to have the ability to deal with unusual situations and to remain calm when things began to go awry.

Besides demonstrating these characteristics, the men also had to possess physical agility and coordination. They had to be over eighteen years of age, with thirty-two the absolute age limit. No one was considered who weighed over 220 pounds. Every candidate was expected to be in good physical condition, "with a history," an army selection paper outlined, "of participation in rugged sports or in a civilian occupation or hobby demanding sustained exertion."

Many of the paras were former athletes, most notably the last two of the battalion's commanding officers. Jeff Nicklin, a superb offensive and defensive end for the Winnipeg Blue Bombers, was also an outstanding lacrosse player. His successor, Fraser Eadie, who was "Nick's" best friend, played junior hockey in Winnipeg and most certainly was headed to the NHL as a skilled defenceman. Danny Cox, a scout with the Chicago Blackhawks, wanted Eadie to sign up with them. When Eadie replied that he was in the Royal Winnipeg Rifles and waiting to be mobilized, Cox told Eadie, "We'll get you out." Eadie, who would become a much respected and admired CO, chose duty before a career in the NHL.

It became apparent after the first major Allied parachute drop, the invasion of Sicily on July 10, 1943, that stamina was actually more desirable than athletic ability. For assaulting paras to be effective, they had to maintain a flat-out performance for at least three days without relief or let-up. This required a capacity to endure hardship, stress, fatigue, and privation. Recognition of this factor early on paid enormous dividends in Normandy, where the battalion's baptism of fire would last for eight gruelling days under attack and the constant threat of being overrun by the enemy.

The army, not surprisingly, looked for emotionally stable personalities who were well motivated and, as the army put it, "relatively aggressive." Volunteers appeared before a three-man selection board drawn from the officers who would be leading the men they picked. Every candidate was interviewed by an army psychiatrist, an interview designed primarily to detect any significant instabilities or dependency on alcohol. The result of this rigid selection procedure was that the army got soldiers of very high calibre, physically fit specimens who, after the intensive parachute training, became without doubt the best conditioned troops in the Canadian Army.

Of all the demanding requirements, motivation was the attribute most cherished by the army — whether the candidate *really* wanted to be a paratrooper. "If it is found that his desires in this direction are mainly those of either conscious or unconscious method of escape from his present situation, or what he thinks his future situation may be, he is a poor subject for a paratrooper," wrote Lieutenant-Colonel J. W. Howard in a memorandum issued by Canadian Military Headquarters in London.

Having passed muster on physical and mental health tests, the para candidates were then subjected to the army's "M" aptitude and intelligence test. John Madden, another Manitoban, like Nicklin and Eadie, recalled that candidates were given a word association test as well, and that the psychiatrist "asked an awful lot of sexual questions." Appropriately so, Madden concluded, having quickly learned that paratroopers were "the most highly sexed group of men I've ever been with in my life." Madden also remembered that, in the course of examination, a piece of onion skin was put on the palm of the candidate's hand to see if he was trembling or sweating.

Naturally, because of the high standards, the quality of the successful applicants matched expectations. This was true in all of the Allied airborne units. A humorous if somewhat misleading account of what a typical British paratrooper looked like appears in *The Red Beret*, by Hilary St. George Saunders. In the book, Bert, a Borstal boy who joined the paras, "looked like the traditional paratroop of fiction. He was thick-set, bow-legged and vaguely simian in appearance. His hair was black and heavily creamed, his lower lip protruded, he looked frankly evil." In fact, the truth was quite the opposite. For some inexplicable reason the paratroop battalions of Britain, Canada, and the United States attracted a host of handsome men, from the top commanders to the lowest private. No one in the British airborne fraternity was surprised, for instance, when Sean Connery, the darkly handsome Scot, was picked to play the role of his countryman Major-General Robert "Roy" Urquhart, commander of the 1st British Airborne Division, in Cornelius Ryan's *A Bridge Too Far* when it was adapted for the screen.

James Gavin, the boyish-looking general who commanded the celebrated 82nd U.S. Airborne Division, and was nicknamed "Slim Jim," presented an image of the all-American boy next door that is still imitated by fashion models today. But the most dashing figure Canadian paratroopers came to know was the ruggedly handsome and cultured Brigadier James Hill, who commanded the 3rd Brigade of the 6th British Airborne Division in which the Canadians served. The Canadian battalion also presented a number of exceptional personalities of its own. The unit's second CO, Lieutenant-Colonel George Frederick Preston Bradbrooke, another westerner, looked every inch a 1930s matinee idol and sometimes acted like one, in the memory of some of the men.

G. M. Kirkpatrick, a neuropsychiatrist at Canadian Military Headquarters, has supplied a number of profiles of candidates whom he interviewed during one selection process in December 1943. One interviewee spent a summer as a roustabout with the Ringling Brothers and Barnum & Bailey circuses. He was a lineman for Bell Telephone and, as a gymnast in high school, had won a medal for tumbling. The man was described as ambitious, alert, and displaying initiative. His résumé showed that he had studied Italian and economics at McGill University in Montreal. This candidate had no problem getting the nod from the attending psychiatrist.

Another man was so anxious to become a paratrooper he was willing to revert in rank to lieutenant from acting major, a sacrifice, incidentally, that many others made, more so in the ranks of the noncommissioned officers (NCOs), who took off their stripes to be accepted. The acting major had been born in England and was educated in France and at the renowned Massachusetts Institute of Technology, where he excelled in rugby and became a member of the fraternity Phi Beta Epsilon. After graduating he took a position with one of America's leading advertising agencies. While Dr. Kirkpatrick thought the man appeared tense during the interview, he assessed him as being "frank and genuine." The clincher that no doubt got the fellow into the paras was a remark he made to the doctor. "I may also wish to find out," the candidate told Kirkpatrick, "whether I have any guts." He was approved by the doctor, who noted in his application that the man was "reliable and a sound individual."

It is useful to review the process of how young Canadians actually got into service during the Second World War. In June 1940, the National Resources Mobilization Act (NRMA) was passed, requiring every male over the age of sixteen to register for national service. Those who voluntarily enlisted, or decided to "go active," in the jargon of the day, became known as "general service" men. They could be sent overseas. The compulsorily enlisted were referred to as "NRMA men" and could not be sent into action. Canadians whose sons, daughters, husbands, and brothers were bleeding on the battlefields overseas came to despise the NRMA men, who were sitting at home leading the good life while their own kin were dying at the front. The NRMA men became known as "Zombies" and, before the war was out, a bitter and divisive debate was waged in Parliament and across the country to decide whether the Zombies should be sent overseas. In fact, on November 23, 1944, an Order in Council was introduced to the House of Commons by Prime Minister Mackenzie King that set in motion government gears to get the Zombies overseas. By war's end thirteen thousand of them had reached Europe, but by the time they had been integrated into the fighting regiments, most of the blood-letting was over. The mere mention of Zombies today evokes bitter memories in many veterans who saw action.

As it turned out, the candidates for parachute training had in effect volunteered twice, in the first instance to go active, and in the second to join the battalion. The reasons they joined varied from getting away from a CO who was a martinet (although they never admitted this to the recruiter) to simply wanting to get a chance to fight, said Canadian paratrooper Dwight Green. Another Green who joined the 1st Canadian Parachute Battalion, George W., cited the same reason. "Parachuting appeared to be an ideal way to enter action," he offered. George Green came out of the war highly decorated.

Lorne Whaley joined for a much more personal reason. His father was a United Church minister, which in his youth had marked Lorne as different from his peers. "Growing up as a minister's son I always felt that I had to do something extra to prove I wasn't a sissy. The paratroopers was the obvious answer," he recollected years later.

Ted Kalicki, an American from Warsaw in upstate New York, ran away from home at age eighteen. In 1942, Americans had to be age twenty-one to enlist in the armed forces, unless the man's parents consented otherwise. After the Japanese attack on Pearl Harbor, Kalicki's father refused to sign the form permitting his son to enlist. Kalicki crossed the border and joined the Canadian Army in Niagara Falls, Ontario. To his dismay he was told that he would have to swear allegiance to the King of England, an act that would forfeit his U.S. citizenship. Kalicki's motivation was so great, he agreed to do so. To his immense relief no one ever approached him to take the allegiance to the King, and Kalicki never brought the subject up again.

Loyst Kelly of Ingersoll, Ontario, joined the paras for a more pragmatic reason. He wanted to pocket the "jump" pay, which, when the battalion joined the 6th British Airborne Division, was two shillings a day. This seemed a lot of money for a fifteen-and-a-half-year-old lad (Kelly had lied about his age to the enlistment officer). When the army found out they had a teenager in their ranks, they assigned him to non-combat duties.

No one was more persistent in joining the army than Costantino "Jim" Gioberti of Hamilton, whose parents had come to Canada from Italy in 1911. His father worked as a tailor, his mother as a seamstress. Despite growing up during the Depression, Gioberti and his three sisters all managed to finish high school. "We were survivors," he said. When the war began, Gioberti was working as a galvanizer at Stelco, Hamilton's giant steel plant, and playing trumpet in a local dance band. Gioberti was what today would be called "street smart." He liked good clothes and he danced up a storm. There isn't a page in his old photograph albums without a picture of the handsome Italian-Canadian with his arm around a woman. He was popular, self-assured, and confident. But his world crashed around him on June 10, 1940, when the first of seven hundred arrests of Italian-Canadians began under the 1939 Defence of Canada Regulations, also known as "The Enemy Aliens Act."

Most of the men were never told what they were charged with. Many spent four years in internment camps under suspicion of being "fifth columnists." After four years no one was found guilty of anything. It was the same month and year the mobilization act became law that Gioberti's father was locked up. The young Gioberti was given a deferment since he was the major breadwinner in the family. But in 1941, angry that his father was interned, Gioberti travelled to Ottawa and made a deal with the Justice Department to join up if they released his father. To his family's delight, Gioberti senior was released from the Petawawa internment camp and was back at the family hearth two weeks later. True to his word, young Gioberti travelled to Brantford to enlist. Anyone who knew or had ever met Jim Gioberti was certain what outfit he would end up in: the paratroopers.

Colin Brebner, of Toronto, was an army surgeon posted to Camp Petawawa on the Ottawa River. One crisp autumn morning in September 1942, all the medical officers (MOs) were ordered to report to the camp's chief MO, a full colonel and a veteran of the First World War. The colonel made his pitch, startling the assembled officers with his candour. Brebner recalls that the colonel was asking for volunteers without specifying what the volunteers would be required to do. He first stated that volunteers must be under thirty-two years of age, not over six-feet-two-inches in height, not overweight, and must have no ear or eye trouble, and no defects in limb. They would be required to take a special medical examination to show they were physically satisfactory for the assignment. He stressed the job was to be a dangerous one, with a good chance of being injured and possibly killed in training or later. He added that he disliked the volunteering business. In the First World War, he said, they had just assigned people to do the jobs. Finally, as a sort of afterthought, he told the men that the Canadian Army was seeking volunteer MOs to serve with a Canadian parachute regiment just being organized. He then dismissed them and asked that those wishing to volunteer let their officers know by noon the following day.

According to Brebner:

We all trooped out of his office and stopped outside the building to enjoy the sunshine and to discuss the whole business. To me it would be a great adventure, but I hesitated as I had been married for more than two-and-a-half years with two small sons, Michael and Gordon, the latter just nine months old. I had read a recent *American Medical Association Journal* article on parachuting and statistics on injuries and deaths. While quite a few people had broken legs, ankles, collarbones, and wrists, the chance of a parachuting death was considered to be one in every seven thousand jumps. Having worked in the camp hospital as a surgeon for years and seeing the number of fractures from vehicle and motorcycle accidents in training, I felt that the odds were really very good for the parachute drops. I listened to the other MOS and heard remarks such as: 'My God, what a waste of a doctor'; 'My wife would raise hell if I even mentioned it'; 'None of us are that stupid.'

Brebner recalled seeing movies where an entire company stepped forward as if one man when asked to volunteer for some suicide operation or other, always with appropriate music swelling in the background. To Brebner's disgust no one had stepped forward. He felt a deep remorse "that in the third-largest army camp in the country it seemed unlikely that there would be a single volunteer." Captain Brebner, who was twenty-nine years old at the time, felt guilty that he had not taken that one fateful step.

His wife, Beckie, and the children were living in a cottage on the banks of the Petawawa River, which ran through the camp. Each morning Beckie rowed him across the river to the camp and met him at night to row him home. As he sat in the boat that night, he studied his young wife and pondered whether or not to bring the subject up at all. After reading the evening paper, he sat pensively studying the falling autumn light when suddenly Beckie asked, "What are you thinking about?" He told her and, without hesitation, Beckie replied, her words sounding like a line of dialogue from a wartime movie:

"Don't worry about us. We'll manage somehow and you should do what you believe you should do." The conversation sounds stilted today, but it was not unusual for patriotic Canadians to talk that way at the time.

The next day, Brebner reported for duty, and within a month he was in Fort Benning, Georgia. On the train as it rumbled through the American South, Brebner reflected on his decision, wondering if indeed it had been rash.

> We had a rather noisy night on the train as everyone seemed to be filled with great excitement and anticipation of the adventure about which we were all curious. I had talked to many of the men, sergeants, corporals and other ranks, and realized the selection of the men was of a really very high standard; most were in their early twenties, very proud of being selected and determined to show the U.S. that Canadians were as good or better soldiers than the GIs. It was obvious that the train had military priority as it never stopped until it reached Columbus, Georgia. Now our great adventure was to start. How well would we all do?

For Captain Colin Brebner it was the beginning of an arduous journey that ended in the most extraordinary way before the first light of dawn on the morning of June 6, 1944 — D-Day. For the others the long march to battle on the green fields of Normandy, in the snows of the Ardennes Forest, and to the very heart of the German Fatherland, this long and often terrible odyssey, began in the pine woods of southern Georgia redolent with the aroma of resin and the occasional hiss of a rattlesnake.

3

"WAHO MOHAMMED, GERONIMO, AND BILL LEE!"

The paratroopers are the tip of the spear.

Lieutenant-Colonel G. F. P. Bradbrooke, commanding officer of the

1st Canadian Parachute Battalion

JUMPING OUT OF AN AIRPLANE IS NOT EASY. THE APPARENT ease with which stunt jumpers, trailing colourful bands of smoke, drop into a football stadium or country fair is deceptive. These aerial stuntmen use parachutes called "steerables," which give them excellent directional control. The 1940s vintage parachutes were primitive in comparison. Besides, trick jumping is very different from a combat jump, where the paratrooper is going out the door at between four and five hundred feet, most likely at night, and carrying so much equipment he

23

almost needs a crane to load him aboard. While the stadium exhibitionist can expect to be greeted with applause upon landing, the paratrooper is likely to meet someone who is trying to kill him.

There were no steerables in existence when the first Canadians arrived at Fort Benning in late August 1942 to begin paratroop training. For most of the soldiers this was their first time outside Canada, and Georgia must have seemed strange if not exotic to lads from the Prairies or the Maritimes as their special train swayed across the rolling hills and plains of this bastion of the Confederacy. They were in the land of peaches, peanuts, and pecans; of Southern women whose speech sounded like pouring syrup. As the train neared Fort Benning the landscape took a different shape. The high plains of central Georgia, with its plantations of walnut trees and red earth, gave way to steep hills and pine forests; hills that could make a cyclist pant and a soldier curse. They'd be on those hills soon enough and they did not look at all inviting.

Benning is located in the southwest corner of the state, on the banks of the muddy and swiftly running Chattahoochee River that separates Georgia from Alabama. Fort Benning was the home of the infantry in one of the great institutions in American life, the U.S. Army. There was a discernible air of the South about the place — sticky heat, soft nights, and lazy days. It certainly didn't seem like an army camp, except for the massive red-brick barracks known as "the Quadrangle," a forceful reminder that this place was dedicated to perfecting the art of war. In the heat and humidity of August, the Canadians found themselves billeted not in those big barracks, but rather, as one soldier described it, "in nondescript, jerry-built hutments, miserably hugging a dusty company street that seemed to run into an infinity of brownish fields totally devoid of vegetation and lying eerily silent, its edges swimming indistinct in the Georgia heat." This was the infamous "frying pan" area of Fort Benning, the assigned domain of every Canadian who took parachute training there from August 1942 until late March 1943.

The course lasted four weeks, based on a syllabus created by the U.S. Army. The original plan was to train fifty new volunteers each week. At first the expected flood of volunteers didn't happen. Someone at the chief general staff soon figured out why. In the beginning the army had decided to allow the NRMA men to join if they wished. To potential volunteers that meant the unit was in fact a home-defence one. If they joined, they reasoned, they wouldn't be going overseas. The status of the battalion was changed, and overnight a flood of volunteers soon began pouring into Georgia.

The training was designated in four stages, A, B, C, and D. The first week (stage A) was given over to unrelenting physical training, PT exercises and long, strenuous route marches. Going to and from the various assignments, they had to run on the double. In the debilitating heat of a Georgia August, this was a torment not to be forgotten.

Stage B saw equally strenuous PT and more forced marches. In between they were given judo lessons and trained in hand-to-hand combat in the so-called judo pits. Brebner, the medical officer, recollected, "Hand-to-hand combat was tough on me as I was partnered with a six-foot-one-inch corporal weighing about 200 pounds to my 165 pounds. One manoeuvre we had to learn was to throw a man so you landed on his chest. He obviously enjoyed toughing with an officer and it took four days after we stopped the hand-to-hand combat for my ribs and chest to feel normal again. The week was strenuous. I ached all over for the first three days, but by the end of the week I was in much better shape and was sure I would manage."

Howard Holloway was certain in his mind that the U.S. instructors were out to break the Canadians. "During unarmed combat training, my instructor seemed to take great pleasure at throwing my 130 pounds to the sand and sawdust just to show me 'how easy it was.' Then it was, 'You all try it on me now!' My back to his front, with his arms around my neck so I could hardly breathe, he said, 'Reach up, grab my shirt with both hands, bring both feet up high, and bring them down hard.' It hurt my stomach, but he made one hell of a poor four-point landing. He said he didn't expect me to do it and wasn't ready, but said, 'Ya'll did good!' I said, 'Big things come in small packages, sergeant.'"

Stage C saw the men learning to tumble and to fall properly after landing. That same week the men got to sit in a dummy airplane fuselage thirty feet off the ground in a parachute harness, with the static line clipped to a cable located above their heads. On command they jumped into space. This is like jumping from a three-storey building and some students found it nerve-racking. They fell twelve feet before being jerked to a stop and then lowered into a pile of sawdust. This was also the week that the would-be paratroopers got to handle a parachute firsthand, which included sixty-four hours of folding and correctly packing what became each man's silk life-preserver. No one dozed through these classes.

The Canadians used T-5 military parachutes. The T-5 consisted of a twenty-eight-foot canopy made up of twenty-eight panels and an equal number of rigging lines, each twenty-two feet long, attached to a webbing of harness fitted over both shoulders and around both legs. As the Canadians were to find out when they eventually joined the 6th British Airborne Division, the British parachutes were similar but the British harness was much superior to the American model. The British harness featured a single quick-release fitting, which made it easier to remove after landing. This reduced the chance of being dragged along the ground in a strong breeze. The idea for the combat paratrooper is to get moving as rapidly as possible once in the drop zone.

The Canadians' first experience harnessed in a parachute came on one of two gigantic steel towers that dominated the Benning landscape, looming 250 feet skyward. Each tower featured four steel arms and a clutter of pulleys and cables, which supported an open parachute. Hitched in a harness below, the soldier was pulled to the very top of the tower and suddenly released. The sensation was described as sensual as the air rushed past their faces and set their parachutes fluttering.

The final stage, D, was the moment of truth, the week the volunteers made five jumps to earn their coveted paratrooper's wings. "Did jumping scare me? Not much! I only lost twenty pounds during four weeks of jump training at Fort Benning. Waiting for the first jump, I kept trying to kid myself that it was fun, but I knew differently," said Henry Fauquier, of Ottawa, who had done a lot of bush flying and prospecting before joining the 1st Canadian Parachute Battalion. "I had often heard that a man's whole life passes before him when he is drowning, but I always figured the story was so much malarkey. But it happened to my brother when he was spinning in a plane out of control. And it happened to me when I stood in the door for my first leap. In a matter of seconds, my mind seemed to click back and I was remembering things that happened when I was three years old."

Sitting in the plane waiting to get to the drop zone (DZ), a lot of first-time jumpers affect smiles. "They think they are smiling," wrote Ronald A. Keith in a wartime training story for *Maclean's* magazine, "but are actually registering about as much happiness as a frozen mackerel." "Thrilling," "exciting," and "exhilarating" were words typically used by members of the 1st Canadian Parachute Battalion in describing their first jump. The truth is the act of jumping out of an airplane is a profound one, most especially in combat.

The American writer Norman Maclean comes as close as

anyone to describing the feeling, as he did in his account of U.S. Forest Service smokejumpers in *Young Men and Fire*. He said that as the plane droned towards the drop zone, all "pertinent pieces of the plane and its universe began to fall into place and become one." He continues:

> Jumping is one of the few jobs in the world that leads to just one moment when you must be just highly selected pieces of yourself that fit exactly the pieces of your training, your pieces of equipment having been made with those pieces of yourself and your training in mind. Each of the crew is sitting between the other's legs, and all this is leading to a single act performed between heaven and earth by you alone, all your pieces having to be for this one moment just one piece. If you are alive at the end of the act, it has taken about a minute — less, if you are not alive. The jump is that kind of beauty when everything has to be in perfect unison in order for men to commit themselves to what once done cannot be recalled and at best can be only slightly modified. It becomes the perfectly coordinated effort when a *woof* is heard on earth as the parachute explodes open within five seconds after the jumper steps into the sky.

Some instructors liked to torment the new volunteers with stories about what happened if you got a "Roman candle"— a parachute that becomes tangled and will not fully open, just trails behind like a candle. If this happened at four hundred feet, they gleefully pointed out, the man would hit the ground in approximately six seconds — not much time to settle accounts. There were lots of jokes about parachuting. One was used in the epic war movie *The Bridge on the River Kwai*. William Holden plays Major Shears, who has been coerced into joining a demolition team headed behind Japanese-held lines. When the leader of the team, played by Jack Hawkins, discovers Shears has never parachuted from an aircraft, he dashes off to check with the experts as to the major's chances of surviving the jump into the jungle. Shortly, he returns, smiling.

"They say in view of the time element they don't think a few practice jumps would be worthwhile," Hawkins's character reports.

"No?" questions Shears.

"No. They say if you make one jump you only got 50 per cent chance of injury. Two jumps 80 per cent. And three jumps you're bound to catch your packet. The consensus of opinion is that the most sensible thing for Major Shears to do is to go ahead and jump and hope for the best."

"With or without a parachute?" Shears snaps back.

The Canadians who trained at Benning and later at Shilo were equipped with emergency parachutes. When the battalion joined the 6th British Airborne Division in England, they had to adapt psychologically to taking the big step with only one parachute. There was no reserve. On learning this, some men didn't like those odds and packed it in, said Andy Anderson. Even with two parachutes, other volunteers just couldn't face that open door of the speeding airplane. Fauquier, who ended up as chief jump master at Shilo after leaving Benning, recalled an incident involving a "lad who looked wobbly as soon as the plane took off. He just sat there with a fixed expression, staring straight ahead, eyes slightly glazed, not even trying to crack a smile while the other boys were making their feeble jokes and breaking into forced laughter. So I kept an eye on him. When the order was given to stand up and hook static lines, he remained seated. When I spoke to him he didn't say a word — just sat there staring straight ahead. Well, we completed the run-up and jumped the rest of the stick. Then, as we circled, I tried to persuade this boy there was nothing to it. He relaxed a little and said he would jump if I would promise to push him out. As we lined up on the target again, he managed to stand up and fasten his static line. But when he moved to the door, he stiffened and froze, refusing to move. His eyes looked as if he were in a trance. So I pulled him back to his seat — that was the end of his career as a paratrooper."

Parachuting isn't for the faint of heart. The ritual that preceded the jump didn't help calm nerves by any means, just increased the tension. It went like this, the commands shouted in a loud voice.

"Stand up! Hook up!" With this each man snapped the end of his static line onto a cable above his head. Three seconds after he jumped, the static line would pull open his parachute.

"Check equipment!" Everyone gave his gear a quick check. Occasionally a wisecracker would tap the man in front of him, holding an unhooked static line (his own), which he had undone, saying, "Is this yours?" This got a lot of laughs.

Next came: "Sound off for equipment check!" To which the paras would respond, "Number eight, ok, number seven, ok," and so on down the line.

"Stand to the door!" or, as the British said, "Action stations!"

Packed like sardines they shuffled forward in unison, keeping in mind their objective of jumping as soon after each other as possible so as to end up closer together on the ground.

"Red on!" This is in reference to a red light near the door. It went on about five minutes before the aircraft reached the drop zone. Invariably, it seemed an eternity that it remained red. When the red changed to green, the stick commander yelled, "Go!" And out they tumbled.

The first training jumps were made at reasonable heights. The first three from 1,500 feet, the fourth at 1,200 feet, and the fifth at 800 feet, which was getting closer to the altitude they would jump in combat, about 400 feet.

Just how fast does a parachutist fall? As Sir Isaac Newton proved, all objects, despite their weight, fall at the same speed. This speed increases at a uniform rate of thirty-two feet per second. When a parachute opens, it offers 450 square feet of silk, which creates resistance almost immediately, slowing the jumper down to a rate of descent of approximately sixteen feet per second. The shock on landing is said to be equivalent to jumping from a five-foot wall or jumping off the tailgate of a truck going ten miles an hour. Paratroopers insist that it seems a greater shock than that. Jumping at four hundred feet, as they did in combat, the parachutist would land in approximately twenty-five seconds. The actual height that paratroopers jumped depended entirely on the pilot carrying them to the drop zone. A pilot trying to evade enemy flak might climb away, as some of them did in the drop into Germany in 1945, exposing the troopers to more ground fire. If, for instance, they jumped at eight hundred feet, they would be in the air twice as long, where every minute seemed like an eternity. American paratroopers prided themselves on being able to exit the aircraft between four and five hundred feet in combat.

When the trooper heads out the door, he is going forward and downward. When the parachute opens, it checks both motions. On landing, the trooper keeps knees and feet together, effecting a side roll to ease the shock. Some troopers got cocky after a few jumps. John Madden remembers a buddy jumping in front of a group of brass at a demonstration jump, flapping his arms and caw-cawing like a crow. Some smart alecs took the leap holding their noses as if jumping into a swimming pool.

Did they yell "Geronimo"? Apparently not, according to Andy Anderson. "That was a lot of American B.S.," he said. The 1st British Airborne Division by all accounts did have a battle cry,

"Waho Mohammed." This shout was supposed to have been inspired by an experience in North Africa. A British para unit, the story goes, was holed up near Sidi Nasr Allah in Tunisia and noticed that villages in their area communicated to each other by shouting across the valleys. It seemed that each message began with "Waho Mohammed." The British peculiar brand of humour thought this a riot; hence, the paratroopers adopted the chant as their own. Cornelius Ryan, in his account of the Battle of Arnhem in *A Bridge Too Far*, described a dramatic scene of the besieged troopers fighting amidst fire and rubble, firing their Sten guns from their hips and shouting "Waho Mohammed." It was suggested the Canadians take a bit of each of the battle cries to make up a Canadian chant, such as "Waho Geronimo!"

There is another story that the American paratroopers who jumped on D-Day emitted a special call in memory of the man who was considered the father of the U.S. airborne divisions. His name was Major-General William C. Lee and he had been sent to England as the commander of the 101st U.S. Airborne Division. Shortly after his arrival, Lee suffered a heart attack and was shipped back home. His successor, Maxwell Taylor, wanted to come up with some kind of tribute to the square-jawed Lee. He urged them when they jumped on D-Day to shout their founder's name: "Bill Lee!" At any rate, it seems the Canadians didn't have a battle cry, other than an expletive or two.

One Canadian who didn't get the chance to yell a chant in battle was the 1st Canadian Parachute Battalion's first CO, Major Hilton Proctor. He was killed on his first jump at Fort Benning. Proctor was from Northern Ireland but had grown up in Canada. When the war broke out, he was an engineer with Bell Telephone in Ottawa. Proctor was killed when he was hit by an airplane. The army told his widow that the collision with the aircraft certainly killed him instantly and that he was dead when he hit the ground. There was a rumour that the plane that hit him was carrying news photographers assigned to get pictures for Canadian papers. This has a ring of truth to it since it was the Canadians' initial jump. Today if anything like that happened there would be a bevy of lawyers on the case demanding an investigation. The U.S. Army flew Proctor's body home to Uplands Air Station, where Proctor's father-in-law received the flag-draped coffin in the drizzling rain. Proctor's wife couldn't be found. She was visiting someone in Quebec when all this happened. Back at Benning the accident certainly must have left the troops somewhat unnerved. Still, they carried on jumping and got their wings about the same time Proctor was being buried back home.

The man who replaced Proctor as co was the most unlikely-looking candidate to head a battalion of paratroopers, who already were being ballyhooed by the press as "aerial Tarzans" and the "supermen of the skies." He was thirty-three-year-old Lieutenant-Colonel George Frederick Preston Bradbrooke, whose friends called him "Brad." He never used any of his given names but always went with the initials G. F. P. Ronald A. Keith gives us a fine description of Bradbrooke in his *Maclean's* article:

You might expect to meet a man of bulging biceps, barrel chest and a booming voice. Instead Lieut.-Col. Bradbrooke is of normal stature and of rather slender proportions. His conversational manner is genial rather than belligerent. This soft-spoken soldier blends infectious enthusiasm with the wisdom of a seasoned jumper. Analysing the paratroop job with an accountant's precision, he says: "There has been a lot of newspaper guff about the glamour of the paratroopers. That's all wrong. We are just fellows who are interested in doing a certain type of specialized job and we have been fortunate enough to be selected. Of course there are special risks.

The paratroops are the tip of the spear. They must expect to go in first, to penetrate behind enemy lines and to fight in isolated positions."

Keith went on to say a paratrooper was tough without being a tough but when his training was finished "he has the hard resiliency of India rubber, wildcat agility, a surplus of ingenuity and, of course, guts." A little hyperbole was natural during the Second World War to boost morale.

Bradbrooke was born in Saskatoon, studied accountancy at the University of Saskatchewan, and when war broke out was working for a farm implement company in Regina. He joined the Saskatoon Light Infantry, took part in the commando raid on Spitsbergen, visited Russia, and volunteered for the paratroops. He took his jump training in England before going to Fort Benning.

Bradbrooke came from a distinguished military family. His father, G. H., was also a lieutenant-colonel and was highly decorated (he was awarded the Military Cross and the Distinguished Service Order) for leading a daring daylight raid in France in 1916 in which two hundred of the enemy were killed or taken prisoner with only six casualties among his own troops. Bradbrooke grew up listening to exciting tales from his first cousin Gerard Renvoize Bradbrooke about life in the famed Khyber Pass, guarding camel trains from marauding bandits. This Bradbrooke left the British army and rose to be a brigadier-general in the Canadian Army.

G. F. P. Bradbrooke as late as 1993 mused that all this military history in the family didn't have any "real influence on me," as he put it. After Bradbrooke led the battalion into D-Day, he was reassigned to administration duties, which everyone said was his forte. Camp Shilo would not be available for almost another six months, but the battalion had to be structured, companies formed, and the American training syllabus adapted once back in Canada for the Canadian climate. With the help of Jeff Nicklin, promoted to be Bradbrooke's second in command (2ic), they set about the task.

The pace of training intensified as the number of troops increased. Jeff Nicklin's wife, Eileen, moved to Georgia to be near her husband. She rented a small room in a boarding-house in nearby Columbus but recalled seeing very little of Jeff because of the arduous training schedule. Columbus then was a very plain city, with wide streets and buildings with fake storefronts giving the town the appearance of the Old West, but instead of cowpokes sauntering down the main street, there were only soldiers in khaki. The main drag was called Broadway, and the other streets 5th Avenue and so on, just like New York. There were a couple of movie houses and some United Services Organization (U.S.O.) dance canteens, but that was just about it.

The real action was not in Columbus, but across the Chattahoochee River in Phenix City, Alabama. The town was a collection of bars, strip joints, and liquor stores. "Life was one of Riley," said Gioberti. "I was made an instructor and given acting-sergeant rank. Nightly we went into town. The girls simply loved us paratroopers, especially Canadians, to the envy of American soldiers." John Madden remembered that, when he was taking the jump training, one of his men was knifed to death in a barroom brawl. There were always fights — U.S. paratroopers fighting the infantry and not infrequently the Canadians. When there was no one left to fight, they fought among themselves; any slight was enough to get the dukes up.

The officers couldn't really go to these joints. They were welcomed at the Fort Benning Officers' Club, which served good steaks, washed down with rum and Cokes. There was a tradition among officers after receiving their wings to be treated to a notorious drink called the "Opening Shock," named for the moment the parachute opened. It was a tumbler half-full of corn whisky and half-full of vodka. When Colin Brebner's time came to down the dangerous concoction, he did so to the amusement of the American officers standing around. When no one was looking, he slipped out to the washroom, made himself bring up, and then headed back into the club. He did this a number of times, remaining sober while the Americans became drunker. His ruse was never uncovered, and word spread quickly around the camp that the "red-headed doctor sure can hold his liquor." Brebner concluded he had upheld his country's reputation, even if he had cheated.

Just before Brebner's drinking bout, Prime Minister Mackenzie King had taken to the airwaves to implore Canadians to embrace temperance as a contribution to a total war effort. King told his radio listeners that the consumption of spirits, wine, and beer had increased 37 per cent since war had broken out. "Those who indulge themselves too frequently and too freely will break under the strain," King warned. To cut consumption King said the government was going to prohibit the advertising of "spirituous liquors" for the duration of the war. In any case, temperance was not the pledge taken by paratroopers.

By March 23, 1943, training wound up at Benning, and the 1st Canadian Parachute Battalion headed home for leave before reporting back for duty, on April 15, at Camp Shilo, Manitoba. All told, approximately 621 Canadians had completed the course. Just before leaving for Camp Shilo, there was a call for volunteers to join the 2nd Canadian Parachute Battalion then training at Fort William Henry Harrison outside Helena, Montana. This battalion had become part of a joint American–Canadian combat unit known as the First Special Service Force and made up a little more than one-third of this international force. Some of the men answered the call. The unit went on to serve in operations in Kiska in 1943 in the Aleutians, and later fought near

Monte Cassino in Italy. It also saw action, the only Canadian force to do so, at Anzio, and took part in the advance on Rome. The unit's last operation was the assault on the south coast of France. It was disbanded in December 1944. Some of its members joined the 1st Canadian Parachute Battalion as reinforcements.

Back in Canada, they started all over again. There never seemed to be anything but extremes at Shilo. In summer it was as hot as the U.S. South, in winter as cold as the Arctic. Bill Jenkins remembered days when they jumped at minus forty degrees Fahrenheit onto frozen ground with no snow to soften the landing. Jim Gioberti summed up the camp in two words: a dump. Homesteaders had reached the same conclusion in the 1880s when they abandoned the area after futile attempts at farming. But Gioberti had more personal reasons for disliking Shilo. He claimed the "Benning Boys" were too often looked upon as being "flashy" by the newly arriving paratroop recruits. Moreover, Gioberti had a run-in with an officer who had him charged with insubordination, stripped of his corporal's stripes, and thrown in the "brig" for two weeks.

Everyone remembers the jump tower at Camp Shilo. The sight of it was a most aggravating feature while on a march. "There was one march pattern of about ten miles to the village of Douglas that seemed exceptionally long as you could always see the jump tower in the distance and it never seemed to get closer on the return hike," said Ed Henry, who had grown up on the Prairies in Shamrock, Saskatchewan. John Madden, who was from the West himself, sensed the wide-open spaces spooked easterners. "I did note the unease, particularly of people from Toronto who encountered the Prairie. They really didn't like it. It made them look around in puzzlement." One thing Shilo made easy was map reading. With the tower as a landmark it was difficult to get lost.

What most remember about Shilo, though, was the rigorous

training. John Feduck, who grew up in Welland, Ontario, was impressed by the quality of the young officers and NCOs, but mostly by how physically strenuous the training was. He arrived as a recruit who went through jump training when Shilo began receiving paratroop volunteers. He was determined to make the grade. Many didn't. Feduck recalled that, when he took the course, 60 per cent of the candidates flunked out and were returned to their units —"RTUed" was the dreaded expression. That number seems quite high, but it may well be accurate, if the obstacle course is an example of how back-breaking the training was. The obstacle course consisted of a ten-foot wall, a twenty-foot drop, a seven-foot-wide water-filled ditch — which had to be cleared in a single leap — a long section of swinging hand-over-hand above barbed wire, a crawl through a lengthy tunnel, up and down a twenty-five-foot ladder, and a dash along the top of a pile of cord wood. All in four and a half minutes.

One of the training courses at Shilo familiarized the men with explosives, such as gun cotton, amonal, prima cord, deto-nators, and grenades, to mention just a few. This course ended with a night drop led by Jeff Nicklin and an attack on a discarded Canadian Pacific Railroad earth-mover, abandoned in a gravel pit. The drop went as planned and the objective was found. After it was rigged with eight hundred pounds of charges, Nicklin had the honour of pushing the plunger. "All hell broke loose," recalled Hew Quick, who took part in the exercise. The blast was so powerful, he said, it blew out the windows of the railway station in the nearby town of Chater, Manitoba. It wasn't until after the war that Quick learned they had blown up the wrong earth-mover. Instead of the abandoned one, they had demolished a perfectly good working piece of equipment.

After the jump training was completed, the troopers turned to small-arms training and specialized courses, such as han-dling Bangalore torpedoes (rockets in long pipes used to clear barbed wire) and hand grenades, practicing on the firing ranges, and taking apart and assembling weapons. There were night marches, day marches, and forced marches. Jumping continued if the weather was good.

The army soon discovered that Shilo wasn't the ideal place for a jump school. Winds were frequently above the fifteen-mile-an-hour speed considered the outside limit for safe parachuting. There was no airfield at Shilo, so everyone had to be sent to either Rivers, Manitoba, an hour's bus ride away, or to Portage La Prairie, a two-hour ride by truck.

Another problem was a most serious one. Having built this rugged, highly trained group of paratroopers, what do you do with it? The infrastructure required to support airborne troops is enormous, and to create one to service one battalion was out of the question. The only sensible thing to do was to attach it to a British airborne division, where the logistical infrastructure was already in place. The 6th British Airborne Division was being formed at the time and it was finally decided to send the 1st Canadian Parachute Battalion to be part of it.

In late July 1943, the battalion was in Halifax ready to board the *Queen Elizabeth*. The future was uncertain and it was with some apprehension that the battalion trooped aboard the stately steamship. What the battalion did not yet know was that fate had cast it on the road to fame under the leadership of an extraordinary soldier whose influence was to be profound on the Canadians he led, a man whom they came to love even though he never promised them anything other than tumult.

4

A SOLDIER'S SOLDIER

War is the province of physical exertion and suffering.
In order not to be completely overcome by them, a certain
strength of body and mind is required.

Carl Von Clausewitz, 1780–1831

S TANLEY JAMES LEDGER HILL WAS BORN MARCH 14, 1911, AT Combe Grove near Bath, into a privileged family, where traditions of duty and honour were valued. James, as he was called by his family, was conscious of war from an early age. His father, Walter Pitts Hendy Hill, was a soldier of distinction who had served in the Boer War and the First World War, service for which he was inducted into the Distinguished Service Order and received other honours. Walter Hill was an instructor at the Royal Military College, Sandhurst. James remembers vividly his father coming home on the eve of the First World War, and announcing "this momentous event."

The boy spent the war years with his mother's family, who owned a number of large farms in Lincolnshire, one of which was commandeered during the war to become Scampton Aerodrome, home to Canadian fighter pilots serving in the Royal Flying Corps. The sweeping expanse of Lincolnshire landscape and the presence of the Canadian pilots doubtless fired a young boy's imagination. Perhaps it was here that Hill developed an affinity for Canada and Canadians.

When it was time to begin school, his parents sent James to Wellesley House Prep School in Broadstairs and then to Marlborough College. Although this was not an army school, his family had deemed that his career was to be in the military, following the tradition of his father's time, when childrens' futures were preordained. The eldest child would go into the family business; the second would manage the family estates, if there were any; and the rest would be detailed to join the services or go out to make a living in the colonies. His father's job was to be in the army, and now so was James's.

I was always expected to go into the army, and I thought that would be my lot. I was lucky because as a youth or teenager we were, in this country, very proud of our great empire, which was the largest the world had ever seen. We also had a king and queen whom we all automatically loved and revered. Today it seems to be the fashion to decry the establishment and the status quo. In our day we had much to be proud of and, as youngsters, very few of us, I think, queried politicians in power, be it Conservative or Labour. Today, things are very different. History is not even taught in many of the schools and clever young men who have no practical experience of what they talk about have joy in decrying the great personalities and leaders of past ages.

James had a brief intellectual flirtation with the idea of becoming a Jesuit, but this was supplanted by reality. A soldier he was to be. In truth, James felt lucky to be at Marlborough College, which he remembered as a hard school with no physical mercy. "To say I enjoyed my time would not be true, but it did me no harm" is how he recalled the experience. There were sports and hunting, which he "thoroughly enjoyed."

In 1929, at age eighteen, James Hill entered the Royal Military College, Sandhurst, to become a student of war, having been passed into the celebrated institution half-way down the entrance list. It was the beginning of the structured and regimented life. Cadets were divided into companies commanded by a commissioned officer, professional NCOs, and corporal cadets. From the very start, competition was strong between the companies, each of which had their own quarters, mess, and billiard room.

The day began at 6:00 A.M., with reveille, and didn't end until 11:00 P.M., with lights out. In between there was a concentrated program of academics and athletics. The cadets studied the arts of war and learned the maxims of war from Frederick the Great to Napoleon; in addition there were practical field classes on envelopment, attack, and defence. There were, too, liberal portions of cricket, gymnastics, and boxing, a sport at which James particularly excelled.

Hill finished Sandhurst in 1931, passing out second in his class and winning the first of many awards, the Sword of Honour and the Sword for Tactics. He was also the Captain of Athletics.

Immediately upon graduation Hill joined his regiment, the Royal Fusiliers. One of England's most venerable regiments, it was founded in 1685, and the colonel-in-chief in the 1930s was no less a figure than King George V. When Hill joined the regiment, his father was its colonel. If that wasn't inspiration enough to excel, there were deeper reasons. Other members of his family had died fighting in this regiment. There was a deep conviction that this was where he belonged. Hill served with the 2nd Battalion of the Royal Fusiliers from 1931 until 1936, when he left to marry. A regimental order, ironically imposed earlier by his father, forbade any officer of the regiment to marry for the first six years after joining. His father wouldn't break the rule, nor did James even contemplate that he should. He took the only course open. He left the regiment, where he was remembered as an outstanding athlete and coach of the boxing team.

James Hill travelled to Southampton to join the family companies of J. R. Wood and Co., and Hill Southampton Limited. The firms owned a number of wharves along the south coast of England and a fleet of fourteen ships called "coasters." These jaunty vessels dashed up and down the coast carrying coal and other goods from the north. When war broke out, Hill was immediately back in uniform, leaving for France in September 1939 with his old battalion of the Royal Fusiliers.

Christmas found him commanding a forward platoon in the Ligne de Contact of the Maginot Line, where the coldest winter in forty years immobilized mechanized transport. Mules and horses replaced them, an odd note to the beginning of the most technological war ever fought.

In May 1940, Hill found himself in Belgium, on the staff of the commander-in-chief Lord Gort, saddled with the task of evacuating tens of thousands of refugees.

This provided a glorious nightmare for some ten days. I remember on May 13 cars were streaming out of Brussels on our main route at 4,500 per hour with a never-ending stream of old men, women, and children, with horse carts, prams, and push carts, along with a good sprinkling of unarmed Belgian soldiers. The only solution was to form refugee parks. No pedestrians were allowed on roads after 3:00 P.M., bicycles and horses 5:00 P.M., and all cars off the road by 8:00 P.M. The German air force, who were completely predominant, soon spotted and systematically bombed and machine-gunned these parks.

The horror of this slaughter remained riveted in Hill's mind, and it was certainly here where he realized that, to beat this enemy, resolve of the greatest depth was going to be needed. When the war began, his mother had said to him: "James, darling, if you are to survive this war you will have to harden your heart."

There was never better advice given to a soldier whose fate dictated he should lead to their deaths the men he loved. The prospect of defeat and the loss of freedom was unthinkable. From the opening days of the war, it was apparent to Hill how great was the responsibility of command. Dominick Graham, in *The Price of Command: A Biography of General Guy Simonds*, defines the onerous life of command. "A commander may acquire expertise from books and exercises. He learns from them that his mistakes will costs lives, perhaps the lives of close friends, and that Hobson's choices will be his daily diet until he cracks, becomes hardened and detached, or simply suffers mentally as his wounded soldiers suffer physically. To experience these things, and never to be able to forget them, is quite another thing. Nothing can condition a commander to their reality but battle itself," wrote Graham. James Hill's test was not far off.

With the German army sweeping across France, the battered British Expeditionary Force staggered onto the beaches at Dunkirk. Hill himself barely escaped, boarding the last destroyer from Dunkirk. He had time to ponder the effects of the Blitzkrieg — most important, the effective use of paratroops in offensive action. In the meantime, because of his success at evacuating civilians from Belgium, Hill was given a cloak-and-dagger assignment. Dispatched to Dublin, he was to advise the Republic of Ireland on evacuation in the event of a German landing on the Emerald Isle. One morning at breakfast, dressed in civilian clothes, he found himself sitting next to a delegation of Germans posing as businessmen, who had, in fact, come to the neutral Republic of Ireland to spy. Ireland never was invaded and Hill returned to uniform. His only pleasant memory as an undercover agent was of two pairs of silk stockings he had acquired in Dublin for his wife.

Hill then made a decision that would change his life. It was about this time that Churchill called for the formation of a paratroop unit. Hill's batman had volunteered to be a paratrooper, pleading with Hill to allow him to go. He did, but jokingly said he felt the loss of the services of his batman to such an extent that he decided to follow him.

By early 1942, Hill was commanding the 1st British Parachute Battalion and found, to his surprise, that the paratroopers were a much more effective bunch of soldiers than regular infantry. Some of his men were wearing the Order of Lenin for service to the Communists in the Spanish Civil War, others wore decorations from Franco for service to the Nationalist side. He also learned something else of the paratroopers' character. "They proved magnificent fighting material provided they were kept on a tight rein and well disciplined," Hill remembered. The battalion had been picked to drop behind Dieppe, but because of uncertain weather conditions they were replaced by commandos. As events unfolded at Dieppe, the "raid" was a disaster, a costly lesson nevertheless for future sea-borne assaults in Italy and Normandy.

The battalion's baptism of fire was in North Africa, where Hill said he learned that the German army was not invincible. In the process, however, Hill was grievously wounded. Coming upon three light tanks dug in on a hill, the Englishman decided to try to capture them. In the moonlight, Hill had noticed small peep-holes in the side of each tank. Putting the barrel of his revolver through the hole, he pulled the trigger and heard the sound of the bullet reverberating around the steel turret. The tank's hatch shot open and the crew leaped out crying "Italiano! Italiano!" and surrendered. Hill crept to the next tank and repeated the performance, with the same results. At the third tank he discovered the peep-hole had been closed, so he banged on the turret with the thumb stick he was carrying, telling the crew to surrender. Suddenly, the turret flew open and out jumped a German, intent not on surrender but on attack. Bullets from his Mauser struck Hill in the chest, neck, and shoulder. Hill remembers firing back at his attacker.

The next thing I knew I found myself looking at three bodies lying on the ground. I recognized the centre one as myself, the one on the left was the German and there was another one on my right. In due course, on coming to, I lifted myself onto my elbows and, sure enough, there to my left was the German and a third body lying on my right. I then had what can only be termed a flash — you need never be *afraid* to die. A great comfort, as I had never anticipated I would live, and, quite frankly a comfort for the remaining years of the war. Having been brought down to my headquarters, I received my second flash: you *will not* die. This was equally comforting. I simply recount these unusual experiences for, if I had felt that the war only consisted of fighting Germans, I could not have survived five and a half years. But I knew life to be very different.

47

Hill's wounds were so severe that the army said it would retire him unless he signed a waiver saying he would never make claim on an army pension. "I didn't join the army to get a pension," Hill told his superiors and signed away any future claims. This was the soldier who was destined to lead the 1st Canadian Parachute Battalion into battle, a man they came to trust with their lives.

After arriving in Scotland, a short leave in London, and records processing at the Canadian camp in Surrey, the 1st Canadian Parachute Battalion was off to what was to become its home base until the end of the war: Carter Barracks, Bulford, on Salisbury Plain in Wiltshire, near the site of Stonehenge. It was here they first met their brigade commander. Six-foot-two-inches, James Hill moved with the nimbleness of a boxer and the carriage of a soldier. Direct, candid, and enthusiastic, Hill exuded energy and confidence. Despite his friendly and charming manner, there was no doubt who was in charge. As the Canadians discovered, Hill was himself a reflection of what he demanded from his officers and men: diligence and commitment.

The 1st Canadian Parachute Battalion was one of three battalions in the 3rd Parachute Brigade of the 6th British Airborne Division. Each battalion consisted of approximately 650 men. The other two battalions were the 8th and 9th. Rounding off the order of battle were two batteries of Royal Artillery and one squadron of Royal Engineers. The 3rd Brigade was unique in that it was the only mixed brigade of British and Canadian troops during the Second World War.

Each battalion had a personality of its own, and as Hill was a shrewd observer of men, he came to use each to its advantage. The 8th were rugged, relentless in achieving an objective, very tough, and not too fussy about detail. This was the opposite of the 9th, who were masters of detail, tackling an assignment only after intensive preparation, and approaching all problems with precision and professionalism. The Canadian battalion displayed all the characteristics of a troop of cavalry. Hill spotted early on in the Canadian battalion a touch of *élan* and elegance in carrying out its assigned tasks; a sparkle and dash that her sister battalions lacked. Hill said many years later:

> The arrival of the Canadians was both a matter of delight and great responsibility. I had been to Canada before the war. I went from Sandhurst to visit the RMC [Royal Military College] at Kingston. I got to know Canada a little and I loved the country. However, this was an enormous responsibility [the Canadians joining the 3rd Parachute Brigade]. They were the only Canadian troops, entirely cut off from their own army. I felt responsible for their lives and welfare and they were a long way from home. I took that very seriously, particularly in the fighting. It was very important that I looked after them and it paid marvellous dividends.

The mixture of British and Canadian troops offered a variety of talent, which Hill knew gave the brigade a wide breadth of competence. The thing he most admired in the three battalions was the fact that all had volunteered; they were men who had joined solely because they thought it was their duty. To Hill this was crucial. Some of them, he sensed, were "spoiling for a fight and in consequence had to be very well disciplined."

From the time of their arrival, the Canadians were in constant training. Although everyone had already won his wings, the men had to go through the ritual again, making five jumps to adapt to British parachute techniques. In preparation for training, the troops jumped from fixed balloons, an exercise that was more frightening than any parachute jump out of an airplane. It seemed an eternity before the parachute opened after the jumper dropped through a hole in the basket suspended below the balloon. The Canadians had heard beforehand how three early British paras had been court-martialled for refusing to jump from a balloon. Unfortunately, the British troops had balked while being observed by the press who had been invited to watch training drops. Equally unnerving was the practice of jumping from a hole in the bottom of the fuselage of a Whitley bomber. If the jumper didn't time his exit correctly, he'd strike his chin on the edge of the hole, leaving the aircraft seeing stars.

Wally Vallette was left upset by one incident at Ringway. A British paratrooper whom he watched exit a Whitley bomber was no sooner out of the aircraft than his parachute got caught on the plane's tail wheel. The pilot banked over a small lake or slough that was nearby, hoping that if the man freed himself he'd land in the water. On the plane's third pass, the trooper freed himself but the parachute just streamed behind him, a Roman candle. The man hit the ground ten feet from the water, and was killed. "Needless to say," said Vallette, "seeing this did not improve our confidence in jumping from a Whitley."

Getting equipment caught on any of the aircraft's surfaces was always a danger. Dwight Green remembers watching a drama unfold over Carter Barracks. A British paratrooper was seen still attached to the end of his static line, his body being smashed against the fuselage. After any number of frantic moves to free the fellow, the plane headed to the coast of the Channel, where they cut the man free, hoping he would survive the drop into the water. He didn't. "It was a very disturbing event for paratroopers to witness," Green recalled.

A story going around told of a gathering of the brass, including Winston Churchill, who arrived at Ringway to watch a jump. The controller of the program was hooked up to loudspeakers so the dignitaries could hear his conversation with the pilots. After some delay, the spectators were startled at the exchange:

"Hallo, formation leader, are you ready for take-off?"

"No," came the reply. "Five of the chaps have fainted."

The Canadians preferred the British parachutes to American ones. Although the canopy was the same size as the American models, the British parachutes had a softer opening and the harness was less likely to bruise arms or legs. The instructors at Ringway were competent and cheerful. The Canadians didn't spend much time at Ringway, just long enough to qualify, before returning to Bulford.

At Bulford the para training was different from regular infantry battalion training. The 1st Canadian Parachute Battalion was made up of four companies, A, B, C, and Headquarters. The last consisted of a small administrative section and three specialist platoons, machine-gun, mortar, and the PIAT (projector infantry anti-tank) platoon. The PIAT weapon launched a three-pound anti-tank grenade up to one hundred yards. Hill put great store in becoming 100 per cent proficient with these weapons, stressing what he called "fire effect," namely, learning to concentrate fire on enemy positions with accuracy rather than volume. Being a boxer, there was another Napoleon maxim on war that Hill understood. "War," said Napoleon, "is like a bout of fisticuffs: the more blows you give, the better it will be." Hill refined this tactic, insisting that the blows being struck must be accurately landed.

The amount of time the battalion spent on the rifle and other firing ranges is evident in the battalion's war diaries. Typical were these entries in early February 1944:

9 Feb. Warm and clear all day. Regular training carried out all day. A Company spent the afternoon on rifle

ranges. 10 Feb. Warm and clear all day. A Company fired small machine-gun on the 30 yard range in the morning. B Company carried out battle drill all day. C Company fired large machine-gun on ranges all day. 12 Feb. Training was carried out as usual with B Company on rifle ranges and C Company doing a forced march in the morning and holding a sports parade in the afternoon. Mortar platoon went on an all day exercise.

There was always the threat of a soldier being weeded out if he did poorly on the ranges, especially in the use of a personal weapon. It is astonishing to read the list of weapons carried by the division. Sten and Thompson sub-machine-guns amounted to 6,504; rifles, 7,171; and pistols, 2,942, just to cite a few of the weapons listed in the division's inventory. Besides mastering their own particular weapon, be it a Sten gun, tommy-gun, Bren gun, or Vickers machine-gun, a cadre of the battalion was trained to handle and fire the enemy's weapons.

Hill believed that simplicity was paramount to success in battle. "We were a very simple organization, dependent on our ability, physical and mental, with the minimum of transport and weapons and therefore no clutter." He instructed everyone to read French names on maps phonetically. There was just no time for French lessons. Instead of boys from the Prairie trying to get their tongues around a word like écureuil, for instance, they'd read it as "ee-cur-il."

Another Hill tenet, after fire effect and simplicity, was what he called "control." The battalion must control the action rather than having always to react to the enemy's initiative. Even on defence, that defence had to be active, always probing the enemy, knowing where he was, what he was up to, and most important, because his own battalions were as different as chalk from cheese, the characteristics of a particular enemy unit or formation the battalion was facing.

Hill's final and fourth principle of war was speed. Not surprisingly he earned the nickname "Speedy" because of his own agitated gait and his insistence on "moving across the country twice as fast anyone else." If his commanders or men could not measure up to these exacting standards, "they might as well pack their bags, put on their bowler hats, and go home." The gruelling marches attest to the priority that Hill gave to rapid movement. Anyone who failed to meet these standards was transferred out of the brigade. The test was a severe one. A formation had to cover fifty miles in eighteen hours, with each soldier carrying a sixty-pound pack and a weapon. Ten-mile marches in two hours were common.

The day began with a two-mile run with Jeff Nicklin, at that time still 2ic, who usually finished first. These morning runs became a bone of contention between Colin Brebner and Nicklin. During a stretch of bad weather, an unusual number of men began appearing on sick parade. The medical officer figured they were catching colds while standing around waiting for breakfast at the end of the runs. He pointed this out to Nicklin in two memos but nothing changed. When Brigadier Hill noticed the increase of sick-parade cases, he called the battalion MOS together for an explanation. When Brebner told him the sequence of events, Hill asked, "You've recommended this be discontinued?"

"Yes," Brebner replied.

"They didn't follow your recommendations?" Hill asked.

"Correct," said Brebner.

Thereafter the morning runs were cancelled on cold, rainy mornings. Nicklin, said Brebner, never talked to him again. "Nicklin was tough as hell. He expected everyone to be as strong and as fit as he was. He'd drive them to the limit," the medical officer remembered. Nevertheless, it was Hill's firm belief that physical fitness saved lives in battle and enabled men to better survive wounds. The brigadier was certain his own longevity was extended by his physical well-being when he was severely wounded in Africa.

Another skill the Canadians had to acquire was unique to British paratroopers. They jumped into battle carrying kit bags attached to their legs. The trick to learn was to keep it attached until twenty feet from landing, at which time the trooper unhitched the bag, which was on a twenty-foot rope. The bag would hit first, in effect acting like a brake and softening the trooper's landing. If the bag became detached too soon, it could begin twirling the paratrooper in circles. So, timing was everything. These bags, which contained various equipment, were dragged off the drop zone and stashed at a company's rendezvous on the edge of the DZ.

Exercises and the so-called schemes were constant from November 1943 to May 1944 — each designed to hone the paratroopers' many skills. Companies were regularly sent to London and Southampton to be trained in street-fighting techniques. Hitler's Luftwaffe had seen to it that there was no shortage of ruins in which to practice house-to-house fighting.

To make these street-fighting courses more realistic, Nicklin asked Andy Anderson, whom he considered an expert in explosives because of his training in the engineers, to rig the bombed-out houses with booby traps. Using detonators, fuses, and prima cord, he set about his work. The combination resulted in a loud explosion, with a little bit of dust and plaster being spread around. As Nicklin and Anderson watched the men going through the rubble, firing live ammunition and tossing live grenades, one section of the men charged up the stairs of a house. Suddenly there was a deafening explosion and the men were blasted back down the stairs in a shower of dust and debris. Someone shouted to Anderson, "I think you've killed them all!" Actually they were just stunned. Nicklin rushed towards Anderson, who was expecting to be reprimanded for the explosion. Instead Anderson heard the CO say, "Now that was a real lesson, good work!"

There was a great emphasis on night fighting and moving rapidly at night over unfamiliar territory. Everyone, too, had to learn to swim, with the battalion taking over the local baths at Yeovil as a training pool.

The Canadians became a familiar sight in the district as they marched smartly across this bleak landscape. John Feduck's memories of Carter Barracks and the district are grim ones. "We were in a desolate place. The training was so severe you wanted to quit. But most kept going. Their objective was to break us so we would quit. But again the comradeship and being distinctive as a paratrooper was great. So whatever they gave us, we took it."

Dwight Green's memory was similar. "It was a very bleak and somewhat desolate area of England. The largest town was Salisbury, which was twelve miles away. The fact that the buses quit running at 9:00 P.M. left very little time for entertainment. Except for the food, the living conditions were equal to or better than some camps in Canada at which I was stationed. Even the weather was better than that of Prince Rupert, B.C. The rock salmon that was served was actually dogfish, much to my chagrin."

Ted Kalicki, the American, offered fonder memories of Carter Barracks. "It was in the area of the country steeped in history.... Stonehenge and the Roman burial mounds were a real treat to me because I always liked history. When would I ever get the chance to be in that area had it not been for the war?"

Hill was aware of the stress being imposed on the troops and, in the hope of making the most of their limited leave time, the brigadier arranged with British Railways to put on a special train running from Bulford to Andover to connect with a fast train into London. Given the wartime priorities on transport, this was some accomplishment, leaving Hill rather pleased with himself. But one Monday morning, a visibly shaken and angry stationmaster from Salisbury was ushered into his office. It seemed that two Canadian paratroopers returning from London had crawled along the top of the train in the pitch-dark and neatly dropped two primed grenades down the engine's funnel, demolishing part of the engine. The vandalism angered Hill, but in due time he got over his disappointment with the unruly Canadians and came to dine out on the story for years to come.

There was another entertaining diversion that occurred in February 1944, a little-told episode that featured Major Jeff Nicklin in a leading role and brought notoriety to the 1st Canadian Parachute Battalion, and to Canada as a country. The event, a football game between Canada and the United States, had its origins over a quiet drink in a private London club.

5

A DIFFERENT KIND OF VICTORY

We beat the sons-of-bitches!

The Honourable George Hees on winning the U.S.–Canadian football match,
White City Stadium, London, February 13, 1944

IN LATE DECEMBER 1943, DENNY WHITAKER, FORMER quarterback for the Hamilton Tigers, was in London for a week-end leave. After the pubs had closed in the early afternoon, Whitaker repaired to one of the so-called private clubs that flourished in the city during the Second World War. Anyone could join by signing his name and paying an initiation fee. The clubs provided the opportunity to drink twenty-four hours a day.

Whitaker, a major with the Royal Hamilton Light Infantry, was sitting quietly by himself in one of these clubs when an

American officer, also alone, sat down at the same table. His name was Eisonmann, a lieutenant in the U.S. Army recreational services.

According to Whitaker, Eisonmann "mentioned the Americans had just brought over to England six complete sets of equipment for football teams. I said very quickly that I knew a lot of Canadians who had played football in Canada and were now serving in the European theatre." After a couple of drinks, Whitaker and Eisonmann agreed that it was "a great idea" to have a match between Canadian and American servicemen, providing the Yanks were willing to equip the Canadian team.

Whitaker approached Lieutenant-General Ken Stuart, the general commanding Canadian Military Headquarters in London, whom Whitaker knew well from Royal Military College (RMC) in Kingston. Within days a formal meeting was arranged to work out details, with representatives from both sides meeting on December 29. It was a cordial gathering as the parties set some ground rules. The first half of the game was to be played under American rules with American referees, and the second half under Canadian rules with Canadian referees. Each side promised to send the other a copy of their rule book. The width of the field was set at fifty yards rather than the greater Canadian width. When American rules were in force, there would be only four men in the backfield, but under Canadian rules five men were allowed (the fifth was called "the flying wing" or "tailback," a position that is no longer part of the Canadian game).

In fact there were many significant differences that, upon examination, seemed to favour the Americans. While the American rules haven't changed all that much since the 1940s, there have been great changes in the Canadian game. For instance, at that time blocking was allowed only five yards past the line of scrimmage. A touchdown counted five points in the Canadian game, as against six in the American. Under Canadian rules, on the kick-off no opposing player can come within five yards of the receiver unless he is onside. In the American game, the receiver can be tackled immediately on the spot by any man.

The Americans were confused by the rule that a ball kicked from a punt formation and into the end zone must be run out. If a team fails to run it out and is tackled in the end zone, one point is scored, called a "rouge." In the U.S. rules, the ball is automatically brought out at the twenty-yard line and is scrimmaged from there. Canadian rules said blocking backs cannot block past the line of scrimmage and that a lineman can block only five yards.

Despite the differences the sides said they felt comfortable with each other's rules and set a time and date. White City Stadium, ordinarily a site for greyhound racing, was picked as the field. The date was fixed for Sunday, February 13, 1944, with kick-off at 2:45 P.M. The Americans were called the "Pirates" and the Canadians took the name "Mustangs." There were to be massed pipe bands at half-time, when a collection was to be taken and donated to the British Red Cross.

Whitaker, excused from duties, moved quickly to round up a team. It was apparent as he ran down the list of names of possible contenders that he had an impressive and talented group of players, including Major Jeff Nicklin, the former Winnipeg Blue Bomber star, and another Bomber, Andy Beiber. From the Toronto Argonauts came Captain George Hees, who played centre, along with George Meen, Ken Turnball, Ron Grant, and Fred Brown. Whitaker felt lucky to get Huck Welsh, one of the country's greatest punters, who had played for the Hamilton Tigers and the Montreal Winged Wheelers, and Orval Burke, who had quarterbacked the Ottawa Rough Riders to a Grey Cup. Whitaker was pleased to see what was really an all-star east–west team taking shape on paper. There was also a sprinkle of college players, Nick Paithouski from Queen's University being one. The coach was Major Chick Mundell, a doctor in the Canadian Army Medical Corps, who had coached Whitaker at RMC All gathered at Aldershot, where accommodations were arranged and practice began. Whitaker laughed when he recalled it years afterward. "We practiced extensively every morning and afternoon and spent the evenings many times drinking beer over at the Queen's Hotel at Farnborough, which actually didn't do our condition much good, but we had a lot of fun."

Authorities were uncertain how many fans would show. By kick-off there were an estimated thirty-five thousand people in the stadium. "On game day we arrived at the White City Stadium feeling pretty optimistic about our chances. I guess we were in a minority in that respect," Whitaker said, "because the odds were fifteen to one for the Americans. They got much better pay than we did. A Canadian private was paid only thirty cents a day, a captain six dollars, so the betting was very heavy and the Yanks were willing to lay the odds."

The first half was played by American rules and ended scoreless. American fans were restless and apprehensive, but a spectacular half-time show by the Canadian pipe bands led by a huge St. Bernard took their minds off the game for a while.

While the narrower field was thought to be a disadvantage for the Canadians, it was otherwise. The Canadians opened the scoring five minutes into the third quarter with a converted touchdown by Ken Turnball, the ex-Argo, a play that no one would even attempt to explain to the British. An American intercepted a pass, fumbled it, and watched the ball dribble over the goal line, where Turnball pounced on it.

The Americans came back quickly in the third quarter to tie the game. With the opening of the fourth quarter, the Canadian Mustangs hit their stride. Burke heaved a twenty-yard pass to Whitaker, who scampered over the goal line for an unconverted touchdown. The ex-Ottawa pivot scored again with seconds remaining. The towering Jeff Nicklin speared the pass on the one-yard line, stepping over the goal line just as the whistle blew, giving Canada a sixteen-to-six victory.

The Canadians in the stands went wild. With the odds the Americans gave, the victory meant many of the Canadians had won more money in one afternoon than they had earned in a year. "In fact," Whitaker said, with a laugh, "days later Canadian soldiers could still be seen through London in battle dress yelling, 'We're number one! We're number one!'" Nicklin, Whitaker, and Burke were singled out as the game stars, and Whitaker took possession of a magnificent silver teapot for the Canadian team as the winners of what was called "The Tea Bowl Game," a prize still in his possession today.

The Americans were mortified by the humiliating defeat and almost immediately demanded a rematch. To Whitaker's surprise, Lieutenant-General Stuart agreed, sending out a memo to get the Canadians fired up for the second game. "I am most anxious that the Canadian Army should field as strong a team as possible for our return match with the U.S. Army. We are having considerable difficulty in fielding as strong a team as we would like," Stuart wrote. He asked whether certain officers could be made available, naming three men, one of whom was Nicklin. Stuart's office was informed shortly that Major Nicklin regretted he was not taking part in a second game, citing concern over possible injuries, a risk too great in face of the invasion of France, which everyone knew was probably only months away.

Ironically, having put duty ahead of sport, Nicklin was injured four days before the return match was scheduled and could not have played even if he had wanted to. Playing in a football game between officers and men at Carter Barracks, Nicklin was heavily tackled and suffered a broken right collarbone, a fracture painful enough that doctors gave him a shot of morphine before releasing him for duty.

A second game was played March 19, without Nicklin, and again at White City Stadium, drawing a crowd of fifty thousand spectators. The Americans won the match handily. In the memory of George Hees, who played in the second game, they had brought in "ringers" from units around the world, including a former player from the Philadelphia Eagles. "The first time I went to the line of scrimmage," Hees recalled, "I came face-to-face with this guy with a deep suntan. Remember, we're in England and this is March. They'd brought this guy in from Hawaii. So we lost. But the first game? We beat the sons-of-bitches!"

The 1st Canadian Parachute Battalion was far from the cheers of White City Stadium when the second football game took place. They were back in the field at Bulford, training under the worst weather conditions they could remember. Even so, the specialist platoons — machine-gun, mortar, and PIAT — were constantly on the practice ranges, as were the rifle companies. Physical training was stepped up with increased cross-country runs and forced marches. Most of the battalion members made two parachute jumps in March and the battalion was inspected by the commander-in-chief of the 21 Army Group under whom they would serve in the coming invasion.

In April the tempo of training was speeded up for the "operation everyone felt was not far away," noted the diary. Special courses continued with street fighting in Southampton, and intensive swimming courses back at the Yeovil Baths. The entire battalion spent three days in lashing rain and high wind on field manoeuvres near Brighton. A large number of reinforcements arrived from Camp Shilo and were turned over to the training company. The last line in the war diary for

March spoke volumes: "The battalion started to bring itself up to full war establishment."

Although no one knew in April 1944 exactly where the invasion was to take place, the Allied chiefs had already selected Normandy in June 1943. Normandy was less defended than other possible sites, there were enough suitable beaches to land the invasion force, and, most important, there were beaches that were within flying range of fighters based in England. Moreover, the landscape behind the beaches was suitable for rapid construction of forward airfields once the push inland began.

The Canadians were unaware of the amount of squabbling that was going on with the higher brass on how best to use airborne troops in the invasion, beginning with Churchill himself, who was unhappy with the number of planes available to transport the paratroopers. Air Marshal Leigh-Mallory expressed grave concerns about the dropping zones of the 82nd and 101st U.S. airborne divisions on the western flank of the invasion forces, citing experience gained in Sicily, where it was found that flying over well-defended areas usually resulted in high casualties. He judged that only 30 per cent of glider-borne troopers would ever reach their objectives.

There was ample evidence that Field Marshal Erwin Rommel, charged by Hitler to stop any invasion attempt on the beaches, was rapidly fortifying the beaches and more ominously installing his so-called Rommel's Asparagus, wooden poles dug into the ground on all likely glider landing zones. The Germans had just launched a massive campaign to teach ground forces how to deal with airborne invaders, going so far as to issue a detailed colour booklet on what tactics to employ when facing enemy paratroopers. The Canadians, and for that matter, all of the Allied planners, had yet to learn just how much the hedgerows would impair the invaders fighting in the *bocage* country of Normandy. These hedges of stones, roots, and earth, built up by local farmers over the centuries, were near impenetrable.

On May 24, 1944, the battalion left Carter Barracks for its assigned transit camp at Down Ampney, in Gloucester. The 1st Canadian Parachute Battalion had been in England for almost a full ten months, during which it had undergone the most intense training to produce a group of highly skilled and superbly fit men. In a few days these Canadians, whose average age was twenty-two, would face the rigours of combat in an enterprise of such complexity, destruction, and mystery that it would change their lives forever.

6

D-DAY

Jumping is the most irrevocable commitment anyone can
make. There is no going back.

Corporal Dan Hartigan, 1st Canadian Parachute Battalion

SOLDIERS GOING INTO BATTLE AREN'T EXACTLY AS EXUBERANT
as Rotarians heading to a convention, remarked S. L. A. Marshall, the American military historian. After the first Allied airborne assault in Sicily, they were even less so. Some military
thinkers questioned the feasibility of large-scale drops, citing
the experiences of American and British paratroopers in Sicily
who were widely dropped behind the invasion beaches and far
from their objectives. Worse, many of the planes carrying the
parachutists were shot down by their own side. What saved the

Sicilian operation was that the drop was partially botched in the first place. The scattered troops led the Germans to believe that there was an overwhelming force of paratroopers, a dispersion that actually contributed to the success of Operation Husky. The Germans spent too much time tracking the paras when they should have been concentrating on the beaches, where the main force was dragging itself ashore.

Until this first major Allied drop, there was plenty of debate over whether paratroopers should be dropped a safe distance from an objective, or directly smack on top of it. Sicily proved that it was better to hit the objective directly and suffer the casualties that were bound to occur rather than land farther away and fight your way to the objective. Sicily also proved how important it was for the pilots and crews charged with getting them to the drop zone to be well trained and rigorously disciplined not to stray from course when met by a heavy concentration of enemy flak. Most of all, D-Day planners had concluded that the successful delivery of a large airborne force on the continent "is dependent, almost completely, on the efficiency of the so-called pathfinders," those paratroopers who preceded the main jump to set up navigational and other homing devices to make sure that the main body of the paras jumped at the right moment and landed in the right spot. What the Canadians weren't told was that invasion planners were willing to risk higher than normally expected numbers of casualties by allowing the paratroopers to jump, if need be, in thirty-mile-an-hour winds rather than the absolute cut-off wind speed of twenty miles an hour. A file in the 21 Army Group invasion plans said, "if essential 30 mph could be accepted but casualties from dropping would be considerably increased."

The objectives handed to the 6th British Airborne Division for D-Day were really quite formidable. The division was to be dropped east of the Orne River and the Caen Canal that parallels it. This was the left flank of the main British assault force landing on Sword Beach at the French seaside holiday town of Ouistreham. It was a vital piece of landscape, especially the crossroads known as "Le Mesnil." The 1st Canadian Parachute Battalion was picked to defend and hold this key objective after its initial objectives were achieved. The crossroads sat on the high ground that overlooked the beaches at Ouistreham. To lose it would be disastrous.

Before digging in at the crossroads, however, C Company was handed the most daunting task. The company would jump with the pathfinders of the 22nd Independent Parachute Company, making Canadians among the first of the Allied invaders, a fact that has long faded from memory. Once on the ground, C Company was to secure the drop zone, called "V" on the invasion maps, so the pathfinders could set up the navigational and homing devices to bring in the main body of paratroopers, approximately an hour later. Once the DZ was secure, C Company would move towards Varaville, a small hamlet near the DZ, where a German artillery headquarters was located. This was to be put out of action. The next objective was a small radio and signals station west of the DZ. This, too, was to be destroyed. The final objectives were to blow up one bridge just east of Varaville, on a small tributary of the Dives River, called "the Divette," and a second bridge east of the village of Robehomme. All of this was to be accomplished with just 110 men.

With the DZ in Canadian hands, in would come the rest of the 1st Canadian Parachute Battalion along with the sister battalion of the 3rd Brigade, the 9th Battalion. Its ominous task was to take out the four guns of the Merville battery that sat perched in an enormous bunker of concrete above the invasion beaches. A Company was assigned to protect the 9th Battalion's left flank on its march towards the battery and to hold off any

German assault launched against the 9th Battalion as it went about its mission. The final objective given to B Company, or part of it, was to blow up another key bridge at Robehomme, four miles south and east of Varaville. This bridge on the Dives River was most important. To knock it out was to deny the Germans a vital route on which to mount a counter-offensive against the beaches.

The 3rd Brigade's 8th Battalion was to drop approximately seven miles south of where the Canadians dropped. They were assigned the task of capturing three bridges, two at Bures and one east of the town of Troarn, and to hold them until sappers of the 3rd Parachute Squadron arrived to blow the bridges. If these objectives were accomplished by the 1st Canadian Parachute Battalion and the 8th Battalion, all the bridges over which the Germans might counter-attack would be denied them. And the successful storming of the Merville battery would assure a safer landing on the beaches for the seaborne invasion troops, timed to land just at daylight.

The 6th Division's other brigade, the 5th, were responsible for numerous objectives west of where the Canadians operated, including the capture of two key bridges over the Caen Canal and Orne River by a small *coup de main* party in gliders. The *coup de main* party was led by the redoubtable Major John Howard and his men of the Oxfordshire and Buckinghamshire Light Infantry, the "Ox and Bucks," as they were called, who would later perform one of the most extraordinary feats of the D-Day landings.

At least one paratrooper thought the Canadian objectives "important, exciting, and dangerous, but there was also an air of romanticism about them." Twenty-year-old Corporal Dan Hartigan of Sydney Mines, Nova Scotia, likened the assignment to other dashing raids against the Germans that had taken place in France, the Western Desert, Norway, and Italy. The Canadian objectives, he thought, would "rank up there with the best or the worst of them, depending on how you looked at it."

Brigadier Hill remembered that, when at first glance the objectives seemed unrealistic to accomplish, they were in fact not so.

Looking back on my brigade's task for D-Day, I think I would have accepted it was well nigh impossible when two thousand young men with an average age of twenty-two, who, with the exception of three officers, had never seen a shot fired in anger before, were asked at the dead of night, in a foreign field, to put out of action an enemy battery and destroy five bridges interspersed with deep irrigation ditches and German wire. These tasks covered a span of seven miles. Thereafter, as near first light as possible, the brigade was required to capture and hold the ridge, which was the dominating feature overlooking the Orne Valley, where the main divisional objective was the capture intact of the bridges over the river Orne and canal so that a bridgehead for a future breakout for 21 Army Group could be established.

When regarded in retrospect and the cold light of day, that was a formidable task in all circumstances. The extraordinary thing was that no one of us doubted our ability to carry it out. During our months of training, we had built up faith in each other and faith in ourselves.

Another British parachute soldier, Lieutenant-General Sir Michael Gray, wrote that, when the fiftieth anniversary of D-Day was celebrated, the accounts of that momentous day all described the events as unfolding in a precise, neat and tidy way, with everything going according to plan. "In fact, of course," he said, "it was not like that at all, and it was the airborne practice of detailed, individual briefing for every officer and man that made it work. Each was trained to use his initiative when things went wrong. A parachutist fights a lonely battle. He has not a real front or rear, he often feels he is fighting the battle on his own, but by dint of training, and sometimes by sheer guts, precarious situations were turned to our advantage."

Colin Brebner, the MO, was very impressed by the thoroughness with which all the Canadians were briefed. It was only after the battalion arrived at the transit camp at Down Ampney that it found out where it was going and what tasks had been assigned to each company and individual. Brebner remembered that "morale of the unit was high, as was the physical and mental condition of the men picked to go." After a year and a half of training for some of the men, they were anxious to finally get into battle.

The atmosphere at the camp as D-Day approached was a strange mixture of tension and downright relief. At last they knew where they were going and there was a restlessness to get moving. This mounting drama was played out against a backdrop of frenzied activity and amidst a setting of impermanence. There were few buildings in the transit camp. Everyone lived in tents. There were no bowling alleys or swimming pools there. Instead, the presence of barbed wire surrounding the camp and armed guards spoke of the gravity of the situation. It was the same throughout southern England at these makeshift transit camps, which had sprung up almost overnight in the spring of 1944. As the days passed, the tension grew.

Brebner wrote about the transit camp in his diary.

Almost immediately we were taken into the briefing rooms where surprisingly detailed sand tables had been prepared, showing the areas of our battalion objectives. Low-level photographs taken by Mosquito bombers had been blown up to at least six feet by eight feet showing in detail the drop zone, the nearby village of Varaville, and the edge of the field where the power lines limited the DZ and rendezvous points.

It was amazing to see cows in the fields, the power line which was at the far end of the DZ, and people on the roads. All other ranks were completely briefed, and those fighting men who had specific objectives were taken into the briefing rooms by their officers to repeatedly go over the details of where they should rendezvous and what to do if they appeared lost on landing.

To Ted Kalicki's horror there developed a distinct possibility that there would be no landing for him. One of the battalion's officers called Kalicki to the orderly tent and, after asking about his family in Warsaw, New York, suddenly dropped "a bombshell" on him. "He told me that he had all the papers ready for me to transfer to the U.S. Army. Due to the fact that I had not sworn allegiance to the King, there would be no obstacle to the transfer. He then said that by the time I was moved to a U.S. unit and went through basic training, the war would be over. I really admired him for that magnanimous gesture but I vehemently refused. I told him that my whole purpose in enlisting was to get into combat and not to avoid it."

After the first four or five days, despite continued training and continued questioning regarding the roles of each soldier, men began to get impatient. When the beer and spirits in the mess ran out after eight days, the men became more restless. A fight had broken out between two paratroopers, one of whom was knocked unconscious and didn't come around. Brebner was called and, after examining the man, he believed him to be suffering a concussion. The doctor recommended that he be removed to the nearest military hospital, where he could get proper round-the-clock treatment. The precautions that were set in place to prevent a breach in security were nothing less than remarkable. In Colin Brebner's words:

> On entering the hospital, as I had been instructed leaving the patient and the driver in the ambulance, I asked for the commandant that I might talk to him privately. The injured soldier had of course been briefed and knew when and where in France the invasion was to take place. I, a captain, rather embarrassed, laid down the instructions to a full colonel. The man must be isolated in a single room with a W.C. attached. One nursing sister must be detailed to his care and remain incommunicado in the room with him at all times. The colonel himself must be the only medical officer to see and care for him and, if X-rays were necessary, be in the X-ray room with him with strict instructions not to talk to them or allow anyone other than the colonel to enter. This was to be continued until the commandant received word that the man could be taken out of isolation. I was amazed at such contingencies, but realized how easily a feverish patient could start talking and let the cat out of the bag.

The MO's next task was an equally important one, imposed on him by James Hill. Brebner was to take the empty ambulance to the nearest brewery and fill it up with beer, ale, cider, and whatever hard liquor he could lay his hands on. This he did with delight. "I was wondering if the springs would hold the load as we returned to the transit camp with the ambulance filled to the roof. I was greeted on my return with enthusiastic volunteers to unload the ambulance," recalls Brebner.

* * *

On June 3, 1944, the weather turned extremely hot. A sudden violent thunderstorm hit the camp, threatening to destroy the models and photo enlargements of the battalion's objectives. Later the battalion was transported to the airfield nearby, where the men drew and fitted their parachutes. These were left in the aircraft, mostly C-47s or what the British called "Dakotas," one of the most remarkable aircraft, military or civilian, ever built. Each parachute was placed in the appointed stick where each man was to jump and marked with the last two digits of the trooper's serial number.

The next day was fine and the soldiers couldn't understand why the delay was necessary, not knowing that the seas on the Normandy coast were too rough for landing. That day the RAF crews who were assigned to carry the Canadians to the drop zone came to camp, where they were introduced to the sticks they'd be flying into battle. The battalion diary notes that the "pilots' calm certainty of dropping their sticks at the right time greatly reassured the men," words that would come back to haunt the battalion. The entire division was addressed by its colourful commander, Major-General Richard Gale, know to the men as "Windy," naturally enough. "The Hun thinks only a bloody fool will go there," he told them. "That's why I'm going!" The remark was greeted by the men with a rousing cheer.

Brigadier Hill spent the last day at Down Ampney visiting his battalions, and generally giving pep talks, one of which ended with his famous and rather prophetic line, "Gentlemen, in spite of your excellent training and your splendid briefing, you must not be daunted if chaos reigns. It undoubtedly will!"

Hill pitched his tent that day in the area where the Canadians were bivouacked and was struck by how energetic he found them on the eve of battle.

This period was very interesting to me. All day long the Canadians, with whom I'd pitched my tent, were playing games, baseball, throwing balls about, and I thought what tremendous vitality these Canadians have got. Then in the afternoon I would visit my English battalions and find half a dozen chaps desultorily kicking a football, and the rest asleep. I thought to myself, here is the difference between the Old World and the New; the *élan* and *joie de vivre* of the New World of Canadians, and the maturity and the not worrying, not bothering and having a good nap while you can, of the British.

June 5, 1944, dawned cloudy with a light wind. Quickly word spread that the jump was on. Everyone was ordered on enforced rest during the morning and the afternoon. As the sun set, the men dressed and loaded up. It is astonishing that they could walk after this final exercise. Ted Kalicki recalled:

I have thought many times of what we had carried with us on that drop. My memory is pretty clear on that point. I had sewn two bandoliers of .303 rifle ammo onto the bottom of my Denison smock and I also criss-crossed two more on my shoulders. We had felt bags strapped to our legs, which we could release with a rip cord and then lower away from us on a 20-foot nylon cord. The bag held our .303 Lee Enfield rifle, more .303 ammo and some phosphorous grenades, several sticks of plastic high explosive, a couple of two-inch mortar shells and several hand grenades. In our back packs, we had a change of underwear, socks, three days' supply of field rations, which consisted of tinned corn beef, hard candy, cigarettes, razor, a plastic tube in which we could put the PHE [plastic high explosive] and make a Bangalore torpedo;

one or two No. 74 anti-tank grenades, prima cord and whatever else we could stow and felt we could carry. We couldn't climb into the aircraft on our own. There were two men, one on each side of the door who literally lifted and threw us into the plane.

Kalicki forgot one item. All the paras carried a six-foot-long piece of rope with a toggle on one end, which they wrapped either around the waist or over the shoulder. For reasons that will become evident, this simple piece of equipment saved many lives.
Hartigan, too, was a pack-horse.

Every man carried two pounds of plastic explosive primed with a screw-cap detonator, a No. 74 anti-tank grenade, several Mills bombs, and, in the assault companies, every second man carried four loaded Bren machine-gun magazines or four two-inch mortar shells, and smoke bombs for covering assaults. They knew that it might be as much as four days before they were properly resupplied from sources which came from the sea, and that if certain highways and road junctions were not taken and held, air resupply might be their only avenue for obtaining more ammunition.

Colin Brebner was equally loaded down as the battalion MO. Two medics were assigned to him, and each man carried the leg kit bag with the twenty-foot rope. The two enlisted men, besides being loaded with ammunition and grenades, carried a stretcher, which they rode out the door and released after their parachutes opened. Brebner carried a map case, binoculars, a Colt .45 automatic pistol, a U.S. Army handgun, battle dressings, bandages, surgical instruments, and morphine.
The battalion's padre, an Anglican priest named George

Harris, carried a few personal belongings, a collapsible altar, and communion kit. Harris was born in England but emigrated to Canada. Quiet and soft spoken, he was popular with the men.

At 7:30 P.M. the battalion was paraded in full kit and began leaving for the aircraft. C Company had already left for RAF Harwell, the remainder of the battalion headed for Down Ampney airfield. At 10:45 P.M. the men began boarding the planes, and one by one the Dakotas fired up. The night air rang with the sound of motors igniting. One by one, the engines kicked in, shaking the fuselages and the ground under their wings.

A reporter for the *National Home Monthly*, Gwenda Thompson, described a moving scene involving Padre Harris.

> As I wandered around the field shouting questions above the roar of revving planes, a sergeant came among the men and said: "Padre wants to know if any of you would like a few prayers before we take off?" The chaplain, G. A. Harris, was waiting with a prayer book in his hands. His face was daubed with camouflage paint, he wore a green jumping smock and there was a crash helmet at his feet. The Canadians knelt and, as a stormy sun set over the woods, prayed and sang a hymn. After the blessing they turned, buckled the last straps and filed into the planes.

John Madden attended a Catholic service that evening, a Mass being celebrated by the 3rd Brigade's Irish padre, a priest named McVay. Having learned that the departing D-Day troops had been issued condoms, McVay thundered in a sermon to them to throw away the condoms because they may be going to their deaths "with sin in their pockets." Madden said some of the men were so shaken that, after the Mass, they discarded the devices. Padre McVay was captured by the Germans and sent to a prisoner-of-war camp, but not before setting about to bash his captors with a blackthorn shillelagh given to him by Brigadier Hill.

One by one, then, the planes sped down the runway, disappearing with a growl into the blackness. Inside the planes, each man worked to balance his fear. There was no turning back.

The Canadians in C Company were the first in the air. Dan Hartigan was doing some arithmetic. Military theorists said attacking infantry should have three-to-one odds in its favour. But at the briefings, intelligence reports said there were no such odds like that: realistically it was going to be one-to-one. As the plane rumbled through the night sky, Hartigan studied the men in his section.

> We were loaded to the hilt with grenades, Gammon bombs, flexible Bangalore torpedoes around our necks, two-inch mortar bombs, ammunition, weapons, and water-bottles, which were fractionally lighter. Our exposed skin was blackened with charcoal; the camouflage netting on our helmets was all tied up with burlap rags, and the space above the harness in our helmets was crammed with cigarettes or with high explosive.

When the plane levelled off, Hartigan made his way to the Plexiglas tail section, where he kept up a running commentary for his mates. As they passed over a town soon after taking off, Hartigan was amused to see dozens of people out for a late evening stroll.

Soon they were crossing the Channel. Someone gasped, "For Christ's sake, gimme a cigarette." As the planes throttled back, they knew the jump was near at hand. Below in the pitch blackness, there were shimmering patches of light on the ground. Everyone knew these were the low-lying areas that the Germans had flooded. The aircraft banked slightly to the right. The men were standing now and hooked up, waiting to drop through the exit hatch of the Albemarle bomber. When the red light switched to green, out they plunged into the darkness, the roar of engines, the blast of cold air, and the clang of the equipment ringing in their heads. One. Two. Three. Four. Five. Six. Seven. Eight. Nine. Ten. Out they went. Fast. Fast. Fast. One after another. There was no hesitation. The faster they jumped and the closer together they jumped, the better it would be on the ground.

"In combat, the paratrooper's most pressing moment comes when his parachute opens and he has a short moment to realize that the commitment he has just made is irrevocable. For an instant there is a clear exhilarating feeling of the die being cast, absolutely," Hartigan was later to write.

"Shortly after landing," Hartigan recalled, "we knew that disaster was at hand." The drop zone was being bombed by the RAF, who had overshot the Merville battery. By the time the 9th Battalion arrived above the DZ, Hartigan was in a daze, "stupefied" by the blast of one of the four-thousand-pound bombs. When someone asked where they were, Hartigan replied: "In France."

John Madden's flight began eerily, he thought. As Madden prepared to board the aircraft, he heard Colonel Bradbrooke say, "Goodbye, John." Somehow the words left Madden feeling strange. It was the first time Bradbrooke had ever called him by his Christian name. Madden had taken off from Harwell along with the other members of C Company. As they neared the coast, Madden undid the bolts of the floor hatch in the Albemarle and stared down the English Channel.

With five minutes to go I ordered the men to stand over the hole. I myself took up position kneeling at the aft edge. I couldn't see the warning lights so one of my men was to shout "Red on!" then "Green on!" as the pilot gave the signal. Looking out the side ports I saw flak lazily climb its weary way into the heavens. Through the jump hole I glimpsed the Channel surf foaming against the French coast. Immediately the patchwork quilt of the Norman countryside flashed into view. Above the cold rush of the prop blast I vaguely heard the words, "Green on!" This wasn't right. "Red on!" should have come first. I seized the opportunity to stay aboard the airplane a few seconds longer. Then reason took possession. Either the pilot hadn't put on the red light or I hadn't heard the warning. I screamed, "Did you say green?" Then the shouted reply, "Yes, I said green." So there it was. There was no alternative. I pulled in my arms and pitched head-long out into the night. The parachute opened as it always did. Of more immediate concern, however, was the ground below me, ground unwelcome and unreal. The damp of midnight covered it with a sheenlike mist that shifted in mystical patterns to disclose doll-like farms. I landed in soft pastureland.

Madden later learned that the confusion resulted because both the red and the green light had flashed on at the same time. The few seconds he had delayed in jumping had put Madden down, by his estimations, over a thousand yards beyond the DZ. Equally disturbing was the fact that he had landed two hundred yards from two anti-aircraft (ack-ack) guns that were spewing forth a steady stream of fire. Shortly, he was joined by two of his men. Of the others, there was no sign.

One of them was Nelson MacDonald, who came from an Ottawa family of nine children, a background he thought made him a resourceful person. As the number-six man in the stick, MacDonald found his exit from the aircraft partially blocked by one of the hatch's doors. The man before him had accidentally pulled half the hatch closed when he dropped. MacDonald knew as he tumbled out that those few seconds of delay had separated him from his mates. He recalled seeing lots of anti-aircraft and tracer fire in the distance, but it was relatively quiet as he floated through the darkness.

The bombs that had fallen on the DZ created a gigantic dust ball, confusing the pilots who arrived after the disastrous RAF bombing run. But, for Richard Hilborn, the confusion began long before his aircraft took off from Down Ampney. His pilot, Graeme Metcalf, who came from Wales, noticed that one of the two engines was overheating, dangerously so. Everyone piled out of the aircraft with the faulty engine, tramping to a spare Dakota that was standing by for just such a mishap. "All the parachutists had to pile out of the aircraft, and my crew and all the navigation gear were swept into the other aircraft in a chaotic fashion. We got away as quickly as we could, but I reckon it was about an hour late."

Metcalf's plane, Dakota KG421, arrived over the drop zone at 1:02 A.M. Hoping to hone in on the beacons that the pathfinders had dropped, Metcalf discovered to his disgust that the charts detailing the frequencies had been left behind in the switch of planes. Flying by dead-reckoning, the Welshman dropped to a few hundred feet, hoping to pick up some landmark. All around him the sky was filled with flak explosions and deadly bright arcs of tracer bullets. As Metcalf recalls, "There was quite a party going on ahead, with a tremendous fireworks show, and I saw a Sterling quite clearly as it blew up. I was four hundred yards behind him and flying at about three hundred feet. It blew up right in front of me and lit up the sky. Below I saw the mouth of the Orne River very clearly. Then I knew where I was."

Just before the blast, Hilborn and his men had stood up and

hooked up, ready to go out the open door. "Suddenly, the plane took violent evasive action. About five of us ended up in the plane's lavatory at the back end of the plane in a heap of bodies," Hilborn recollected. Metcalf finally figured out where he was, or so he thought, and signalled the paratroopers, who had now disentangled themselves and were once again poised to jump. Hilborn remembers that he "was absolutely terrified the way the old kite rocketed and bucketed about the sky. I got out OK and the opening shock tore the knee strap off of my leg kit bag. It hung away from me and I couldn't reach the quick release, so I landed with my kit bag attached. I landed in the corner of a field somewhat shaken and to no end surprised. I have never come down faster."

When Hilborn hit the ground, he was still struggling to release his kit bag, in hopes of softening his landing. As was the case for so many Canadians, Hilborn was nowhere near the drop zone. It was only after three hours of wandering with three others, and the assistance of a French farmer, that Richard Hilborn discovered his whereabouts. He had landed a mile and a half northwest of the DZ.

One reason for the scattered drops was that, although the pathfinders had dropped accurately on Drop Zone V near Varaville, the radar beacon and responder units, called "Eureka," were all smashed in the drop and totally useless. A green lamp for signalling the aircraft survived the drop, but because of so much dust and debris kicked up by the wrongly dropped RAF bombs, pilots who were bringing in the paratroopers couldn't see the light. The pilots were left to their own navigational devices on board to get the paratroopers to the drop zone.

Ted Kalicki's drop seems typical of most of the jumps.

The stick that I was in for the jump did not go as planned. I was the next to last man and Ted Evans was the last. As we got to the door of the C-47, the man in front of me went all to pieces and would not go out the door. I don't remember his name and if I did, I would not mention it as it would do no good for anyone. Anyway, I stepped over him and called to Evans: "Are you with me?" and he hollered "Go!" and out I went. Due to the holdup in the jump when I exited the plane, I could see that we had really got separated from the rest of the unit. Five or six seconds delay at that speed and we were really strung out. When I landed, I was all alone. It was about 0100 hours.

Dwight Green was also blown off course.

I vividly remember exiting the aircraft and while descending watching the tracer bullets chasing the aircraft through the sky. I had a very hard landing but suffered no injuries. I landed in an orchard and it was very dark and difficult to see any distance. I eventually managed to gather together five other troopers from my own battalion, plus a corporal from the 1st Special Service Commando Brigade. We were unable to orient ourselves due to there being no visible landmarks upon which we could take a compass bearing. Eventually, we made contact with some 224 Field Ambulance medics. They were able to advise us of our proper direction. It was too late and too far to get to our original objectives so I, as the senior person, decided to go to the rendezvous (RV) at Le Mesnil crossroads.

John Feduck's luck was not much better.

Our transport plane was dodging flak and manoeuvring all over the sky. I heard shrapnel hitting the fuselage but I was more concerned with the green light, which would indicate when I was to leave the C-47. Suddenly, the plane banked sharply, and I fell out! I struck what must have been the largest tree in all of France. A branch hit my head and knocked me out for a few minutes. When I awoke I found myself suspended about ten feet or so from the ground. I soon saw what appeared to be a German patrol walk right up to the tree and some of the soldiers even looked up at me. But they could not have seen me. They moved on and I let myself down by cutting my shroud line.

Completely alone and not knowing where he was, Feduck started walking in the direction he believed the crossroads to be. Passing a house surrounded by a stone fence, he came face-to-face with a German soldier. "I pulled out my Colt .45 and pumped three rounds at him. He staggered and I turned and got out of there." Feduck wandered aimlessly until dawn, when he found other members of his battalion.

Twenty-four-year-old Lieutenant Norm Toseland, who worked in a wholesale hardware warehouse before the war, peered out of one of the plane's windows as it crossed the Channel. He was amazed at the number of ships in the water below.

During the run into the French coast and looking down in the dim moonlight, the fellows saw the Channel alive with ships of all sizes. As the green light came on to jump, it was very hard to reach the door of the C-47 Dakota as the plane bucked and swerved to avoid the ack-ack fire. One of the crew stood at the door to help the heavily equipped paras make their exit and called out, "Good luck!" as each man stepped out into space to come to grips with the enemy. Only two of our men returned to England in the aircraft as they had been wounded by flak during the fly-in. I was the last man of eighteen to jump and when my 'chute opened it became very quiet as the plane's engines faded away. You couldn't see the ground until you hit it or you landed in a tree or on the roof of a building. I fortunately had a dry landing in the back-yard of a farmhouse. We had been badly scattered due to the problems of getting out of the aircraft and some navigational errors.

Eighteen-year-old Mark Lockyer, who had grown up on a farm near Oshawa, Ontario, remembered it took forever to cross the Channel that stormy night. Half-way across, the clouds parted, revealing an astonishing sight. "As far as you could see there were ships," the farm boy recalled. "They seemed so close together, I thought you could walk back to England stepping from one ship to the next. It was an amazing sight and I felt that I was part of something extraordinary. I was very proud."

Lockyer didn't remember much about the actual jump, but the landing was memorable. He landed in the flooded area of the river in water up to his chest. Struggling for what seemed an eternity, the young soldier made it to a tree-lined road in the distance, where he stopped to rest. Suddenly he heard someone breathing heavily and called out "Maggie," the first part of a two-part password, which was the names of two cartoon characters of that era. If the intruder was Canadian or British, the reply would have been "Jiggs." When there was no reply to the chal-lenge, Lockyer slipped the safety off his .303 rifle and was ready to fire, when, out of the darkness, appeared a cow.

The Canadian battalion's first combat jump, so eagerly anticipated after so many strenuous months of training, was developing into an unmitigated disaster. Of the seventy-one Dakotas that left England carrying the Canadian battalion, only seventeen dropped the paratroopers on the Varaville drop zone.

Nine planes dropped the men one mile away, and eleven aircraft flashed the green light one and a half miles from the DZ. Nine sticks of paratroopers were dropped into the flooded marshes on both sides of the Dives River, where many of them drowned because they were so weighted down with ammo, explosives, and weapons.

Colin Brebner made it to the drop zone in the same plane with the man who had not spoken to him since the confrontation over the early morning runs, Jeff Nicklin, the battalion's 2ic. He found himself with Nicklin as a result of one of Brigadier Hill's battle maxims that there must always be two command groups in each battalion. Accordingly, battalion headquarters was split in two. Colonel Bradbrooke took one half of the adjutant, signals, intelligence, clerical, and medical sections in one plane, and Major Nicklin took the other half in a separate aircraft. If one plane was shot down, or dropped the men too far from the drop zone, the second group would take command of the battalion. Brebner had boarded the plane first, so he knew he'd be the last to leave. His recollection of the flight and the drop is gripping.

Our outside view was limited due to the small window ports, but everyone craned his neck around to see vaguely the shapes of planes moving past in the dark. Finally, our plane started to move slowly and turned to follow the preceding planes. After a short period we stopped, the engines roared, and we took off. The plane's noise gave us no clue as to where other planes were and, as I was far forward in the fuselage, the wing obstructed my view out of the small port next to me. We flew for quite a time overland, and suddenly someone said, "My God, we're over the Channel." It was a clear night with some flimsy clouds below us, but we could make out the water below with nothing on it.

Again, after some time, we realized we were approaching the coast of Normandy as in the distance there appeared to be small spots of light dancing upwards in the sky towards us. It was quite beautiful as the spots came apparently slowly and suddenly flashed by rapidly. All at once everybody realized that the spots of light coming were tracer bullets. When I realized this I recalled DC-3s [DC-3 was the civilian designation for the C-47] did not have puncture-proof gas tanks. However, ours did not seem to make any evasive movements and, once past the coast, there were no more "shooting stars."

Suddenly, the red came on and everyone stood up, and hooked up their static lines to the cable attached to the ceiling of the aircraft. Expectedly, the red light went out and the green light came on. There was a lot of noise near the door as men went out . . . suddenly the line of men moving to the rear of the plane stopped and within a few seconds the red light was on again with about 6 of us left in the plane. The horrible thought struck me: "Do we end up back in England?" Fortunately, we had an excellent pilot who made a wide circle and came back approaching the DZ again. Suddenly red to green again and all six exited without difficulty.

Once the parachute opened I once again marvelled at how absolutely quiet it suddenly became and what a lovely night it was. A watery moon was half-way up the sky — the plane with its noise was now far away and I was able to orientate myself immediately, recognizing the Varaville–Le Mesnil road, the power line well off to the south, and the area of the rendezvous — a perfect drop by an expert pilot. By this time, my leg kit bag was swinging gently below me, and the ground was coming up to me quite rapidly. I was just thinking "What a piece of cake," when suddenly I stopped descending. I had not noticed that I was drifting backwards and looking up I found my chute was entangled in the outer edge of an umbrella-like tree with heavy foliage. The trunk of the tree was a good 15 [feet] away. I looked down — a smaller tree top was below me, slightly off to the right side and about 10 [feet] below.

I reviewed the instructions I had received if stuck in a tree. Unload all equipment you can. I jettisoned the rope kitbag by untying the rope; I dropped the binoculars and map case. I tried to rid myself of my service revolver, but it was held too securely under my parachute harness. Next, I climbed up the rigging lines away from the tree trunk. I got up to the edge of the canopy and pulled, but failed to budge it at all. Try to pendulum yourself by alternatively pulling on the rigging lines near and away from the trunk of the tree and try to grasp by hand or legs a branch solid enough to sustain your weight. All I got hold of were small branches that broke off with my weight.

By this time my arms were tiring and from my efforts the seat of the chute had worked its way to just below the small of the back. About this time, firing broke out in the region of Varaville, very sporadic, and I thought what a good target I'd make if someone just chanced to look in my direction. While not panicked so far, I realized I should try to hurry. So, to make a rope of my rigging lines, I cut 3 or 4 of them and tied them together lowering the rope so [I could] feel it had touched the ground then securing the upper end to my parachute harness. Lastly, release yourself from the parachute harness and slide down the single strand of nylon to the ground.

With all the bulk of my camouflage jacket I could not find a place to tie my rope where I could tighten the knots securely. I figured I could hit the quick release after climbing up the rigging lines where I could manage to tie the knot. Doing this my leg straps fell away but something was stuck behind — and hanging by my arms I pulled like mad — the obstruction released and suddenly I found myself hanging by one leg strap. I got my other arm up, and tried to pull myself up hand-over-hand but quickly realized my previous efforts had made my arms almost useless. I realized I shouldn't wait longer as I would get steadily weaker, and decided to drop. I knew heights at night were very deceptive, but thought I could swing into the smaller tree below and at the same time land as for a parachute landing to minimize injuries. I swung to the tree, missed it, and landed on hard ground, a wagon track as it turned out to be.

I was dazed immediately, but got my wits back within a minute or two. I knew immediately my left wrist was broken — although not painful immediately. I lay quietly for a minute or two to regain as much composure as possible. I then felt my thighs — no fractures or pain particularly. I moved my knees and ankles and no sign of damage. I looked up at my chute swinging high above me and realized I had dropped about 40 [feet]. I rolled over on my stomach and, pushing with my right arm, got on my knees and, with much effort, managed to get on my feet. I stood feeling very shaky and as the shakiness eased I took one step only to fall with a crash — fortunately to the right, onto my back again. I knew something in my pelvis had been broken and that I was going to stay where I was. A very rapid twenty minutes had passed. Such a short war.

Colonel Bradbrooke's war was going badly, too. The co found the night drop chaotic. "The problems of getting organized into effective fighting units are immense," he later recalled, particularly so in a night drop. "We dropped about 1:00 A.M., quarter to half moon in plenty of cloud. Many were dropped miles from their actual dropping zone. My particular group was dropped three miles from where we should have been. I landed in marshland in about two-and-a-half feet of water. My batman jumped right behind me and I didn't see him again for three days and then he showed up like a bad penny."

Nicklin also ran into problems when his parachute got caught on the side of a house. He managed to lower himself to safety, even though German soldiers were fighting in the immediate vicinity.

Bradbrooke reached Le Mesnil crossroads when it was still dark. Not long afterwards, Dwight Green arrived with his stragglers. What happened to Green almost immediately shows how much confusion there was. Green arrived at about six o'clock in the morning and reported to Bradbrooke, who instructed him to get a patrol together and root out an enemy sniper who had been shooting at anyone trying to cross the road. Green and his men took off down the hedgerow towards the sniper. They had not crawled very far when someone up in the battalion area opened fire with a Bren gun, aiming in the direction of the sniper. The fire from the Bren was passing just over the heads of Green and his patrol. They were finally able to get out of the line of fire and eventually got to where the sniper had been located. He had gone. Green subsequently learned that one of his own section leaders had come into the battalion area, heard the sniper fire, and decided to fire back. Colonel Bradbrooke had neglected to advise him that he had sent Green's patrol to get the sniper.

James Hill's jump into battle began humorously. He was carrying a football with Hitler's face reproduced on it in luminous paint. The ball was attached to three bricks covered with vulgar expressions. Hill intended to drop this as the plane crossed the Normandy beaches. This he did, to the delight of all the men who saw him heave the ball outside. When his green light flashed on, out he went. To his utter consternation, Hill saw he was going to land in the flooded areas of the Dives River and his thoughts turned to the dozens of tea bags he had sewn into the lining at the top of his battledress trousers, which would be destroyed. Becoming the world's biggest tea bag was not what Hill cherished being remembered for during the invasion of Normandy.

Upon landing, he quickly set about picking up stragglers, many of whom were struggling with their heavy packs in four feet of water. Tying the toggle ropes together, the men began pulling the stranded paratroopers to dry ground. Many of the men who dropped into the river or the flooded areas were never found. Altogether, Hill rounded up a band of forty-two stragglers, including an Alsatian dog named Glen and his handler, a nineteen-year-old private, Emile Corteil.

The para dogs were remarkable animals, of which little has been written. They were actually trained — and never forced — to jump, as well as to detect enemy patrols and to ferret out enemy booby traps. The training of the dog was left to one handler, such as Corteil, who would start off by familiarizing the dog with the interior of a parked Dakota. The dog then was coaxed to jump the six feet from the open doorway. Next, it was taken for rides as the plane taxied around the airfield. Finally, the dog was taught to leap from the moving aircraft when the pilot changed the pitch of the propellers and throttled back. The dogs leaped into action at this sound, just like any of the paratroopers.

With this strange collection, James Hill set out to find the drop zone, growing more furious that he was not with his troops and anxiously wondering how many of the objectives had been taken. It took him four hours to reach the Canadian DZ, where he learned that the bridge east of Varaville had been destroyed.

He was told the fighting for Varaville itself was still going on. No one knew how the 9th Battalion had fared in its task to silence the guns at the Merville battery.

Hill decided the only way to find out was to investigate himself. Leading the forty-two stragglers, he set out for the battery, all of the men wet, cold, and miserable. As they neared the battery, about twenty minutes before the seaborne landings were to begin, the group witnessed a spectacular bombardment from hundreds of ships lying offshore, the softening-up process before the assault boats hit the beaches. As they stood in awe of this incredible display of firepower, a more ominous sound greeted Hill's ears. It was an unearthly, rolling rumble that shook the ground and sounded as if it was coming nearer and nearer.

Hill recalled the terrifying incident:

I had seen plenty of fighting before and I knew exactly what it was. We had got into the middle of pattern bombing by fighter aircraft carrying anti-personnel bombs. We were on a little narrow track with no ditches, water on each side. I threw myself down on the mortar officer of the 9th Battalion, Lieutenant Peters. Here I was lying on top of him and this awful thing went over. Of course, it doesn't last more than twenty seconds. Everything was covered in dust and the smell of cordite and death. It was ghastly. I got on my arms and looked and saw a leg. I knew I had been hit and I thought, 'My God, that's my leg.' I took another look at it and saw it had a brown boot on it. The brown boot belonged to Lieutenant Peters, whom I was lying on top of. He was killed and I was alive.

But only just. Hill was painfully wounded. His left buttock had been sheared off by shrapnel.

Only two of the forty-two men had not been wounded. The scene was a gruesome one. Working quickly, Hill and the fit men tended to the dying soldiers. They injected the seriously wounded with morphine, and collected the morphia from the dead men, passing it out among the living. When there was nothing more Hill could do, he bade them goodbye, and turned and headed towards the Merville battery. Hill recalls that, when they were leaving, "those men, who were all to die, gave us a cheer. That moment will stay with me forever." Among the dead was young Emile Corteil and his faithful Alsatian, Glen. Days later, a burial party led by a chaplain found their bodies, lying side by side in a crater.

Death was everywhere that night. Tom O'Connell found himself in the same plane as Padre Harris. When permission was given to the men to smoke after the plane had levelled off, the men found they were so trussed up with equipment and weapons that none of them could reach his cigarettes. Padre Harris, a non-smoker, produced two packs of Sweet Caporals, and passed them around.

As the plane neared the coast of France, the ack-ack grew intensive. Suddenly the plane shuddered and began to drop. The first men to jump could see that the front of the aircraft was on fire. When O'Connell went out the door, the plane lurched, throwing him against the fuselage. At the same time, he smashed into Padre Harris, who had also just leaped from the burning aircraft. Somehow their parachutes became entangled as they plummeted to earth. O'Connell remembers, "As I kicked the release kit bag, I struck something metallic and a voice came from below saying: 'Take it easy, old man. Whatever you do, take it easy.'" Those were the last words O'Connell heard. The two men crashed through some trees, knocking O'Connell unconscious. O'Connell recalls he "awoke about noon hour and the padre was dead beside me. Our two 'chutes were twisted together like thick rope. I can't think of a braver person than the padre, who, even though we were falling like two stones, was cool enough to caution me to take it easy. Hence I assumed the proper landing position, which saved my life."

It seemed woefully true that chaos reigned, as James Hill had predicted it would. But not altogether. The one operation that exceeded all expectations was the *coup de main* glider assault on the two bridges over the Orne River and the Caen Canal. The bridges were a quarter of a mile apart. It was imperative that they be captured intact before the Germans could blow them up. The bridges were vital in the invasion plans when the time came to break out of the beachhead. Paratroopers were ruled out because of the time it would take them to assemble and march on the bridge. What was needed was a sudden, direct attack that would completely surprise the enemy, one that gave him no chance to blow up the bridges and deny their use to the Allies.

The assignment was given to James Hill's counterpart in the 6th British Airborne Division, Brigadier Nigel Poett, of the 5th Parachute Brigade. A company of the 2nd Battalion, Ox and Bucks, was attached to the 5th Brigade and began training to replicate the enemy successes in Greece (the capture of the Corinth Canal) and Belgium (the glider assault on Fort Eben Emael). Detailed sand models were built, showing the bridges, power lines, houses, down to the tiniest shrubbery. Filmmakers with cine-cameras even simulated the intended flight path so the glider pilots could familiarize themselves with the landscape. The men picked for the attack underwent intensive training, using a similar bridge in the English countryside. On the night of June 5, 1944, six gliders lurched into the air on tow-ropes attached to Halifax bombers, and headed for France.

Staff Sergeant Jim Wallwork and his copilot, Staff Sergeant

John Ainsworth, were piloting the big Horsa glider carrying the leader of the assault force, Major John Howard. They all knew that precision in landing the glider was essential. They had to land exactly at the end of the bridge on the canal. If they over-shot, the glider would crash into a forty-foot embankment. If they landed too early, there was the danger of impaling the glider on fifty-foot trees. Shortly past midnight, Wallwork and Ainsworth unhitched from the tow plane and began a precise descent, the pilot carefully carrying out the instructions from Ainsworth, who with a stopwatch counted down the exact seconds for each of three "legs" of the approach — first, 2 miles; then, 2.3 miles; and, finally, 0.8 miles. Winging in at ninety miles an hour and at exactly nineteen minutes after midnight, Wall-work set the big Horsa glider down in a shower of sparks, in what Howard recalled "was the most hellish din imaginable, the most God Almighty crash." As they neared the ground, the pilots hit a parachute brake, which opened in the nick of time, slowing them down to sixty miles an hour. Had it not, the glider certainly would have hit the embankment. As it was, Wallwork and Ainsworth were both hurtled out the front of the glider still strapped to their seats, which had sheared loose from the bolts holding them to the floor of the glider.

Shortly, two other gliders arrived in a shower of debris. The men in Howard's glider were left momentarily stunned by the impact. When they came to their senses, they leaped from the broken glider to discover that Wallwork and Ainsworth had brought them to within a few yards of the bridge over the Caen Canal, an amazing performance that was later called the great-est feat of airmanship in the Second World War. The canal bridge, which was known as "Bénouville Bridge," was later renamed "Pegasus Bridge" in memory of the paras who cap-tured it. (The paratrooper badge showed the mythical hero Bellerophon riding the winged Pegasus.)

In seconds, Howard's men had stormed the first bridge and overpowered the German defenders in a blaze of bullets. Fifteen minutes later, Howard's men captured the second bridge over the Orne River and flashed the signal that the two bridges were in their hands. That signal was "Ham and Jam," which came over the radio waves as "Ham and Jam, Ham and Bloody Jam," in the words of an excited radio operator.

While this drama unfolded between the canal and the river, a few miles to the east, where the Canadians had landed, confusion continued. As Ted Kalicki got out of his parachute, he tried to make out exactly where he was.

> I gathered in my equipment and as I was getting ready to stand up, I saw a group of men coming towards me. I had no idea if they were friend or foe and my heart was in my mouth. I had my rifle cradled across my left arm and I got a grenade and had a hold of the ring to pull the pin. I was thinking that if they were Germans, I would pull the pin and let go while I opened fire with the rifle. I was really scared and just hoped that I could do what I planned on doing. Of course all of this took less than a minute. They spotted me, and one of them came towards me while the others just stood there with their weapons pointed at me. It was dark and all any of us could see was the form of our bodies. When the one that was coming towards me was about ten feet from me, I was all ready to pull the pin on the grenade and toss it when all of a sudden he blurts out, "Blimey, it's a bloomin' Canadian!" Talk about relief!

The British soldiers, who were most certainly from the 9th Battalion, told Kalicki where the drop zone was. As they talked, Evans, who had jumped just after Kalicki, came up to the group and together they set out to find the drop zone, where, unknown to them, fierce fighting was raging. Only 33 men out of the 110 who jumped made it to the Varaville area. The majority of C Company was dropped west of the Dives River. Exactly how many men fell into the flooded areas is difficult to know. At least three men were never heard of again once out the door of the Dakota. Such was the case of Private Scotty MacInnis, a friend of Cliff Oates. "He was a very friendly, happy fellow who loved plays, music, dancing, hockey, and would give his shirt. He was a roofer and had a dog named Benson. One day, he took the dog up on a roof while he worked, finished and went home, forgetting the dog. That night he had to go back and get a ladder to get his dog down," Oates remembered.

Despite the losses, one group from C Company, perhaps a platoon, quickly took care of the bridge over the Divette. The remaining men under command of Major Murray MacLeod, C Company's CO, attacked a German gun-position located in the gatehouse of a nearby château but came under heavy fire from a pillbox located on the grounds of the château. A Maritimer from Nova Scotia, MacLeod was handsome, with sparkling eyes. Before the war he was a bank teller, but he took to soldiering with enthusiasm, surprising his men and superiors with his professionalism and resourcefulness. Some officers thought Brigadier Hill recognized these attributes and picked MacLeod for the vital assignment of clearing the drop zone and generally cleaning out the enemy before the second wave of Canadian paratroopers dropped from the night skies. MacLeod told John Hanson that he was proud C Company had been picked to go in first. He also said he had had a premonition that he would not survive Normandy. If true, it did not deter his actions in the early hours of the invasion.

Besides the pillbox, there was also a 75mm German anti-tank gun nearby covering the Varaville Road. MacLeod and

Lieutenant "Chug" Walker, an Albertan, along with five men, reached the top floor of the gatehouse that overlooked both the pillbox and the anti-tank gun. The Germans manning the 75mm gun spotted the Canadians, swung the gun towards the house, and quickly pumped two shells into the top floor. One shell detonated a box of PIAT ammunition the Canadians were carrying. The explosion killed four men and grievously wounded MacLeod, who lost the bottom half of his face. He died shortly after being hit. The few remaining Canadians dug in around the town, shooting it out with the enemy soldiers who were trying to reach their German comrades in the pillbox. With MacLeod out of action, the remaining men of C Company were taken over by the colourful Montrealer Captain John Hanson, whose fearlessness was to win him the Military Cross before the day was out.

The success of the storming of the Merville battery was still in doubt. The men of the 9th Battalion who were to take the bunker had, like the Canadians, been scattered to the winds. The battalion's CO, Lieutenant-Colonel Terence Otway, was livid when he discovered that he could muster barely 100 men. The battalion had trained for weeks on a mock-up of the battery assault and had come to the conclusion that to successfully put the battery out of action would require 650 men at the least. Nevertheless, Otway turned and headed for the objective, picking up another 50 stragglers as he went. Along the way, they, like Brigadier Hill's group, came under another misguided RAF bombardment. In a remarkable display of courage, Otway led his impoverished command through the barbed wire and minefield surrounding the battery, charging the bunker itself with guns blazing. At first light, the Merville battery was silenced, and the terrible threat the guns posed to the landing craft coming ashore was now gone. The charge was expensive. Seventy of Otway's men were killed or wounded.

Meanwhile, John Madden, who had also picked up stragglers, was making his way to the crossroads. Coming upon a group of farm buildings, they heard voices, which they suspected belonged to Czechs or Poles who had been dragooned into the German army. Suddenly, a German soldier appeared riding on a bicycle. In the darkness the man mistook the Canadians for Germans and rode along past them. After a short distance, however, he stopped and turned around, coming back towards the Canadians. Madden saw he was wearing the unmistakable soft German field hat and carrying a rifle over his shoulder.

I motioned the men farther into the darkness of the hedge, stood up and again checked my gun. When he was exactly opposite me, I squeezed the trigger and the muzzle spurted fire. At the first burst he turned in my direction. His mouth was open and the moonlight glinted on his teeth, giving the effect of a pitiful smile. The humour ended there. He tried to pedal away. I let him have three more bursts. The bicycle wobbled. With a clatter, he fell and lay gurgling on the road. In the awful silence that followed the chatter of my Sten, we heard the rattle of equipment, the scuffle of feet running towards us. One moment of searing fright and we too were fleeing for our lives, even as the cyclist had tried to flee for his. There is nothing for pride in the way I killed that man; there is nothing for shame in the way we ran. It is of such killings and such threats that regimental history is made, although the latter is seldom recorded or willingly remembered. It wasn't safe to stay in that vicinity and we made off across the fields and along the numerous hedgerows.

Slowly, many of the paratroopers began making their way to Varaville, and none too soon either. The fighting to take the château continued and these new stragglers were warmly welcomed. Troopers from the mortar and Vickers platoons were dropped over a wide area, and it wasn't until daybreak that some of them reached Varaville and joined in the fight.

Marcel Coté remembered being told during briefing sessions before D-Day that "dummies" in parachutes were going to be dropped over a wide area behind the beachhead to confuse the Germans and to make them believe there were more parachute invaders than there were. "I recall our greatest fear was that we would be dropped far from our drop zone. Some even suggested, jokingly, that the last man out of the plane drop a grenade in the tail of the plane, just in case the pilot dropped us in the wrong place." In truth, Coté was dropped many miles from the DZ and captured. Some members of the 1st Canadian Parachute Battalion have come to believe that certain sticks were purposely dropped miles off course to rattle the enemy. Twenty aircraft did drop the men as far as fifteen miles away. There is not, however, documentation in either pre-invasion plans or post-invasion reviews to indicate there is any truth to these suspicions.

Norm Toseland, who was to lead a party farther east, found he had only a handful of men to blow the bridge below the tiny hamlet of Robehomme, perhaps a dozen at the most. He recalls: "It was at this point that a French girl came along on a bicycle. One of our men could speak some French and showed her on the map the bridge on the Dives River. She just left her bicycle and took us over several fields to the river and thus to the bridge. We later learned that she was a French resistance fighter."

More men appeared, some from the mortar platoon and others from the Vickers platoon, so that when Toseland reached the bridge at Robehomme, B Company now consisted of about thirty-five Canadians and about twenty-five others from various units of the division. "We attempted to blow the bridge with the plastic explosives each man carried in his helmet, but we didn't succeed because the charges were insufficient," said Toseland. Mark Lockyer remembered that, while they weren't successful in completely dropping the bridge, they did have enough explosives to drop the centre of the bridge into the water. While soldiers on foot could have crossed the broken span, tanks could not have managed a crossing.

The people who were supposed to bring the bridge down, a group of British engineers, hadn't arrived yet. So Toseland dug in around the bridge and waited. While they waited, three enemy lorries roared up to the bridge on the other side, coming under fire from the Canadians. One truck was knocked out and most of the occupants killed. The other two quickly reversed and sped into the night. Among the Germans was one Canadian paratrooper who had been captured earlier. In the mêlée he managed to escape and join his mates. Finally, the engineers made it to the bridge, quickly and expertly dropping it into the river.

Leaving a small patrol to watch the bridge, Toseland took the rest of the men back to the hamlet of Robehomme, where they dug in around the few houses and barns. Of all the positions, these Canadians had gone the farthest into enemy territory, dangerously exposed to counter-attack. Here they waited, having completed two of the battalion's objectives under the most adverse conditions.

Back in Varaville, the fighting continued around the gatehouse, the château, and the pillbox. Meanwhile, Colin Brebner was still lying helplessly in the middle of the battle. Fortunately, his batman, Bill Adams, stumbled upon the MO and moved him off the track. Brebner instructed Adams to take all the medical equipment to the battalion drop-zone rendezvous. After Adams left, Brebner discovered he'd made a stupid mistake. He had let Adams leave before asking him to administer a shot of morphine. Luckily, Brebner had one syringe of the drug in his own field dressing; he located it and jabbed himself in the left arm.

"The pain was worse in my left wrist, which was badly deformed, but both that pain and that of my pelvis gradually got worse, but remained bearable," Brebner recalls. He lay there as it began to get light. Birds began singing and, to take his mind off his discomfort, he attempted to see and identify them. He had been a bird-watcher from age ten, but trying to see these birds was painful. Every time he turned his head, there was a sharp jab of pain. He concentrated on memorizing their songs, but later he couldn't recall any of them. Shortly, another paratrooper came upon the doctor and, fashioning a stretcher from a garden trellis, dragged Brebner to a makeshift aid post where British medics had collected a number of wounded paratroopers who were being treated by a British MO. Here, Brebner was given another syringe of morphine. He fell asleep, to be awakened by falling bombs.

At seven-thirty in the morning, a German patrol came upon the wounded soldiers. Those who could walk were taken away; the more seriously wounded were left behind. Two British medics got the trellis back into action and dragged Brebner off with the other wounded soldiers. Later, the doctor learned that the Germans used the wounded as a shield to get back to their lines. He was now officially a prisoner of war.

No word had been heard from the 8th Battalion. It too began D-Day disastrously. Many of the soldiers had been widely scattered, and others had jumped over the wrong drop zone. Despite this, a patrol had reached the Troarn Bridge shortly before 5:00 A.M. Amazingly, the bridge was unguarded. Sappers attached explosives to the centre span of this stone bridge and, five minutes after arriving, dropped twenty feet of the span into the river below. About four hours later, another patrol from the 8th Battalion reached the two bridges at Bures, one a road bridge, the other a rail bridge. They couldn't believe it but, again, both bridges were unguarded. Within five minutes these bridges, too, were blown up.

It was shortly after daybreak that Brigadier Hill caught up with the 9th Battalion. To his immense relief and pride, he learned of Otway's success in knocking out all four guns at the Merville battery. A medical officer who dressed Hill's wounds ordered him to get to a main dressing station for further treatment, saying the brigadier "looked bad for morale." Hill exploded. "If you'd been four hours in the water, brewing cold tea, and had lost most of your left backside, you wouldn't look very good for morale either," he said.

Then he set off for Richard Gale's Divisional Headquarters. Because it was difficult for him to walk, someone found a lady's bicycle, which he gingerly mounted, and he was pushed along by a bodyguard. Around noon, he was wheeled up to Gale, who, Hill recalled, "did me the power of good because he said, 'Well, James, I am very pleased to be able to tell you that your battalions have all captured their objectives!'"

No commander was ever prouder of his troops. Against the highest odds, and in the face of heavy casualties, the 3rd Parachute Brigade had been put to the test under the severest conditions and had responded with initiative and courage. Shortly after arriving at Divisional Headquarters, James Hill was under chloroform. When he came to, Hill demanded to be taken directly to his Brigade Headquarters. Piled into the back of a jeep, he sped off looking, by his own account, "rather a mess because I had lost most of my trousers and had bandages hanging out, and, to add to the misery, I had a bottle of penicillin strapped to my side with little pipes going in."

Sniper fire and small-arms firing went on throughout most of the day in and around Varaville and there was heavy enemy mortar fire on the Canadian positions. The local inhabitants pitched in to help the Canadians; women volunteered to dress the wounds of the paras, and men helped in every way they could, as lookouts, messengers, and pack mules. One Frenchman in particular distinguished himself, a note in the war diary tells us. Wearing a maroon beret, which a paratrooper had given him, along with a rifle, the man stalked and killed three German snipers.

By mid-morning the battle for Varaville was over, Dan Hartigan ending it most definitively. The one bunker that held out the longest finally surrendered when Hartigan, firing a two-inch mortar almost horizontally and at point-blank range, lobbed four shells in quick succession. Shortly, a white flag appeared and the Canadians took forty-three German prisoners.

With the objectives in hand, the Canadians now began filtering back to Le Mesnil and the crossroads to dig in for the night, all except Norm Toseland and his men, who were dug in what was virtually no man's land in the hamlet of Robehomme.

John Feduck eventually reached Varaville, where he took part in the assault on the château. John Madden never did make it back on D-Day to rejoin C Company. He spent the first night in France exhausted, asleep in a barnyard with the taste of Calvados on his breath — a gift from a French family who had taken him in at day's end — and far from his battalion.

It took Madden, who had since been joined by Nelson MacDonald and the stragglers he had picked up along the way, two and a half days to reach Le Mesnil crossroads. This included a wild dash across Pegasus Bridge. Although the bridge was in British hands, snipers were zeroing in on anyone trying to cross. One by one, Madden's party sprinted over. MacDonald said he can still hear the "pings" of bullets hitting the bridge's girders as he made his way to the other side. The men lived on a special ration the paratroopers carried, a combination of chocolate, nuts, and cereals compressed into a hard sphere about the size of a tennis ball.

One of the strangest incidents, which occurred a few days after D-Day, was related by Esko Makela from the 5th Platoon, B Company. He remembers that suddenly, from no man's land, came a cow, emitting plaintive moos. It dawned on the Canadians that the cow needed to be milked. Just as suddenly, a soldier carrying empty water bottles crawled towards the cow and began to milk it. There was an almost immediate lull in firing, Makela recalled, saying maybe some of the enemy saw the incident and held their fire. "I like to think so anyway," he said.

Ted Kalicki eventually reached the DZ, mindful of the terrible cost of lives. The first man he saw shot was a fellow named Bastien, who stood up in a field of hay. One shot rang out, and he fell, dead. James Ballingall remembers vividly helping to bury fourteen comrades in the falling light. George Green's recollection, too, was "seeing . . . comrades getting killed and wounded, memories that one never forgets, losing a close friend or friends . . . stays with a person forever."

And this was just the first day.

The Michelin mapmakers apparently found so little significance to the crossroads at Le Mesnil they didn't even note it on their 1944 map of Normandy. The traveller today finds little to arrest the eye, either. Vans and trucks in the service of commerce roar through the intersection of this secondary road that runs between Caen and the seaside town of Cabourg. But if you did stop and take a look around, you couldn't miss seeing the brickworks on the southwest corner of Tuiles Lambert and the company's display of its wares by the roadside. Close by is a small picnic area, and just beyond that a cairn that tells the traveller that Canadian paratroopers defended these crossroads at the beginning of a long crusade, the liberation of Europe from the tyranny of Nazism.

The crossroads are located in the geographical centre of a long, sloping ridge that gently rises near Merville and ends at Troarn. Looking west and north, one can see the Caen Canal and the Orne River, and beyond that the sea at Ouistreham. Whoever held this ridge would determine the fate of those landing by sea. The success or failure of the eastern flank of the invasion hinged on possession of this ridge. It was here that the ragged remnants of C Company assembled after the battle of Varaville, and that other stragglers of the 1st Canadian Parachute Battalion found their way after the wild and chaotic drop of June 6. For the next eight days, the Canadians found themselves under constant bombardment and engaged in primitive hand-to-hand fighting, where only stealth and courage stood between victory and defeat.

As night fell on that first day, James Hill took stock. The 8th Battalion had mustered 280 men; the 9th, which had suffered so many casualties assaulting the Merville guns, was down to 90 men; the 1st Canadian Parachute Battalion counted about 300. In the early hours of the morning of the June 7, the first of many attacks began against the Canadians by infantry of the 857 and 858 Grenadier regiments. Supported by Mark IV tanks and self-propelled guns, the Germans hit B and C companies. Thinking that the paratroopers did not have mortars, the enemy advanced in the open, where they suffered heavy casualties when mortars in the brickyard went into action. One tank got within one hundred yards of the Canadians before being driven off by the PIAT gun. A charge by the Germans was stopped with bayonets by B Company. A captured prisoner told the Canadians the Germans were desperate to capture the brickyard and the crossroads. There were no more attacks that day but there was heavy sniper fire.

In the darkness of night, Toseland and the troops who had dug in around Robehomme decided the position was too untenable and drew back to the crossroads. Later that day, a patrol discovered a nest of Germans in a farmhouse only a few hundred yards away. The men from B Company and Head-quarters Company, led by Captain Peter Griffin, charged the farmhouse, driving the Germans out in fierce hand-to-hand fighting. Mark Lockyer was one of twenty-three men who made the charge.

"Fix bayonets." That's what Pete Griffin said. I thought this was idiotic. I had been to a special battle-drill course and the first thing we learned was not to attack without artillery support and if there wasn't any, you were to abort the operation. I said to the guy next to me, "This is like 1914–1918. Is he serious?" After putting the pig sticker [the bayonet] on, Griffin yelled, "Charge!" Well, we hadn't gone ten steps when guys started dropping like flies. Then I got hit. A machine-gun bullet in the right lung. Down I went. The fighting continued and I could hear the wounded yelling, "Help! Help! Somebody help me!" After the Canadians went back towards our lines, the Germans appeared coming across the field. Two of them came near where I and the other wounded were lying. The one guy looked like a soldier, baggy pants, dirty clothes, but the other guy, an officer, had a pressed uniform, even a shirt that was clean. He went to the first wounded guy, looked at him, pulled out a pistol and "thung"— shot him in the head. Then he went to the next wounded guy and again, "thung." One shot in the head. After he had shot the first guy I reached inside my jacket and soaked my hand in blood from the wound and smeared my face with it. I lay perfectly still and held my breath. I could hear them coming towards me. Suddenly I felt a horrible kick in the stomach. I didn't flinch. Then two more kicks. They moved off. I guess they figured

I was dead. I could hear the third wounded guy crying out, "Help! . . . Oh no!" Then "thung" again. I lay there until it got dark. For a while I passed out because after the Germans left I found a syringe of morphine and injected myself. When I thought it was safe I crawled perhaps one hundred yards back towards our lines. Then I heard someone say, "There's someone out there." I said, "It's me, Lockyer. Don't shoot." One of these guys then asked, "What's the password?" I said, "Christ, I dunno. I've been lying out all day." Three days later I was back in England in hospital. Because of the wound I couldn't use my right hand so I couldn't shave. One day Queen Elizabeth visited and stopped at my bed. I must have been the scruffiest Canadian she had ever seen.

Before the day was out five awards for bravery were won by battalion members. Peter Griffin received the Military Cross, and sergeants J. A. Lacasse and G. H. Morgan and privates R. A. Geddes and W. Noval were awarded the Military Medal. The description of Geddes's action was typical.

At Le Mesnil on 8 June 1944 in a company attack this man with his sniper was detached with a Bren group to give covering fire to his section crossing open ground to the objective. When the company was counter-attacked he and the Bren group were cut off but kept fighting and finally found their way into the company. Twenty-five dead Germans were found by stretcher bearers in the area where this team fought.

The Canadians discovered early on that Brigadier Hill was no rear-echelon general. The lanky brigade commander was constantly in the forward positions and under fire along with his men. "My theory is that all parachute leaders, be you a brigade commander, commanding officer, or platoon and section commander, should always lead from the front, provided you do not lose control of what is happening," Hill recollected. "But, if you are so well organized that you have control of the thing, then you are right up in front. Of course, it was very necessary with the Canadians. They reacted to seeing you with them."

Hill's insistence that they knew who they were facing often brought the brigadier to the forefront. Suddenly, there'd be a rustle, and turning, a private would see his brigadier and hear him whisper something such as: "Well, where are these filthy beggars?" This probing by Hill uncovered the fact that, by June 8, the 3rd Parachute Brigade was up against a first-class German infantry division, the 346 Grenadier Division, supported by tanks and self-propelled guns.

It was common practice for the Canadians to establish what were called "listening posts." They weren't in any designated place. A patrol would creep out at night and get as close to the enemy as possible to try to pick up any tidbit of intelligence, such as the kind of mechanized support a particular unit might have. Bit by bit, the pieces were put together and an accurate assessment was made as to the kind of response the Canadians needed to deal with a situation. These patrols were often heart-stopping. So was duty in forward Bren-gun positions. Ted Kalicki has a vivid memory of one night suddenly being charged by a German with a bayonet who "looked nine feet tall." Kalicki barely had time to raise his rifle, but succeeded in killing the lunging soldier, who fell dead on top of him. There was no quarter given in these hand-to-hand encounters; soldiers could not afford to show mercy when they were fighting for their lives. Treachery, too, was not uncommon among the enemy, as Norm Toseland discovered to his regret.

The war ended for me about 4:00 A.M. on June 10. Until that time I had led a rather charmed life. I had seen many men killed and wounded, but, for me, only shrapnel through my trousers. It all happened when I was returning to battalion headquarters with some of my platoon from a reconnaissance patrol when a German staff car came up the road heading for our lines. We immediately hit the ditch and shot up the car, which crashed into the ditch. A voice called out in broken English from the back of the car. He said he was a friend, wounded, and to please help him. I waited for a few minutes and then crept along the ditch. I called out to the man that I was going to get him out of the car. He would be my first prisoner. I stepped out on the road about 30 feet from the car. I was met by a burst of machine pistol. Two bullets in the abdomen. I dropped and rolled into the ditch and the boys poured more shots into the car, finishing the guy off. It would be a long time before the boys would take prisoners.

The issue of shooting prisoners is a sensitive one, a topic that veterans think best not discussed. Brigadier Hill said in all of his wartime experience he was never aware that any of his men shot prisoners. To a man of such *noblesse oblige*, this kind of conduct was unthinkable. Yet, two days after Toseland was shot, a patrol from A Company ambushed a car carrying a high-ranking propaganda officer. He was brought back alive, but three others in the car — a Gestapo officer, a sergeant, and a driver — were killed, according to the battalion war diary. The next day another staff car was ambushed by a B Company patrol and all the occupants were killed. When the car was searched, the Canadians found that one of the dead men was a paymaster who had 38,000 francs in his briefcase.

The same day, a patrol alerted the battalion that two

companies of enemy soldiers were forming in front of A Company, ready to launch a sneak attack. Artillery was quickly brought into action, inflicting heavy casualties on the attacking Germans.

Reading the battalion's war diary all these years later, it is astonishing to see how constantly the Canadians were under enemy fire, perhaps the most debilitating effect of war on soldiers, whether it be mortar, artillery, or tank fire. There is a deep sense of helplessness in lying crouched in a slit trench or an earth bunker. The thunderous roar and rumbling of the ground tests the steeliest of nerves; wondering where the "next one" is going to land can send men to unimaginable depths of despair and terror. It is equally terrifying to be strafed, to see the plane bank towards you and the little bursts of fire coming from the guns in the wings. What really angered the Canadians was when they were strafed by their own planes, as they were twice in Hill's memory. On one of the strafing runs, RAF Typhoons raked a château next to Hill's brigade headquarters, killing the pregnant wife of the château's owner. According to Hill, "Our doctors tried to save the baby, to no avail, and we buried her in a shroud in her garden with what dignity we could muster under such circumstances. Soon after that the husband and housekeeper left and my brigade headquarters occupied the château."

It is difficult to know how many Canadians were killed by so-called friendly fire, fatal confusion being the bane of warfare. In the Gulf War, for instance, 24 per cent of the Americans killed, 35 men out of 146, were mistakenly shot by their own comrades. Such incidents are not confined to recent conflicts. In the American Civil War, a Confederate sentry shot his own general, the redoubtable Stonewall Jackson. This may have been what happened to Company Sergeant-Major G. W. Embree on June 10. Bob Sullivan, the young soldier from Oregon who had joined the Canadian parachute battalion, was part of a team ordered to rout out a nest of Germans.

> Our platoon was chosen to clear a small area of houses along the road leading directly away from our lines. We had our meeting for instructions just before dusk and by the time the lead part of the platoon had moved out it was dark. It was my understanding that Embree was to remain in the platoon's original position.
>
> Blackie LeBlanc and I were to bring up the rear of the attack carrying the small 2" mortar. As the platoon moved out we fired off one round that Blackie had aimed towards the crossroads that was our objective. As luck would have it, in the dark the round hit an overhead power line forcing the round down and it exploded practically on top of us. Blackie thought he was hit (and he may have been, but not enough to stop us from joining the attack). When we finally advanced up the road, the platoon had moved on. . . .
>
> All hell was happening up the road, Blackie and I were fired upon from the area between buildings on the left side of the road. Bursts from automatic weapons were being fired right at us. Both of us fired in return, fell to the ground and threw grenades in the direction of the enemy fire — we moved along the road joining the remainder of our platoon at the crossroads.
>
> Our mission to clear the area was evidently successful and we then returned to our original positions. The next day we were informed that Embree was found dead in the same general area where Blackie and I had thrown our grenades and answered the automatic fire at us with our rifle fire.

Jeff Nicklin, still Bradbrooke's number two, was wounded on July 23, 1944. He tripped a wire that set off a land mine, which the battalion had rigged as a booby trap. Shrapnel ripped into his arms, legs, and buttocks. He was evacuated immediately to hospital in England.

John Madden accidentally shot himself during a mortar attack by the Germans. He dove into a slit trench, and in the process pulled the trigger of his gun, shooting himself through the hand. Another man in the trench yelled, "You goddamned fool, you nearly shot me!" The hand became so infected and smelled so strongly that Madden stuck his hand out the window of the vehicle taking him to the aid station to get the wound treated.

On June 12, the enemy nearly broke the line on the ridge. On that day the astonished Canadians saw Brigadier Hill charge the German lines, carrying what appeared to be a shepherd's crook and looking remarkably like a biblical figure. The Germans had mounted a do-or-die attack at the crossroads where the Canadians were dug in, and farther down the line, where the Black Watch was in position. The German attack soon broke the Black Watch, who began retreating. This left only a small contingent of the battered 9th Battalion to stem the flow. Colonel Otway radioed Hill to say he didn't think he could hold off the Germans without help. At this news, Hill ran to the crossroads, where Colonel Bradbrooke gave him his reserves. This was C Company, commanded by the fearsome John Hanson, an officer whom Hill particularly admired. Hill always looked in a man for what he called "fire in his eyes." Hanson passed this test with high marks. "John Hanson was a very tough Canadian. He really was an iron man, a splendid chap but a very hard nut."

"It was hard to understand Hanson," remembered Fraser Eadie. "He was about as crazy as they came. But he was fearless, absolutely. I would see him on leave in London and I couldn't understand why he was out of jail. He was hammered most of the time on leave. His guys would do anything for him because he had the guts of a canal horse on anything. And as a fighter he was just spoiling for trouble."

As Hill and Hanson set out to reinforce the 9th Battalion and the Black Watch, an eighteen-year-old Canadian soldier dashed up to Hill and said, "Sir, I'm going to be your bodyguard." Hill thought this most noble. The young man was Ray Anderson, a Metis from Alberta. Carrying his Sten gun, Anderson fell in beside Hill and off they went, but a few minutes later a mortar blast seriously injured Anderson in the right shoulder and left leg and he was unable to continue.

With Hill and Hanson in command, C Company was powerful enough to turn the tide. The enemy retreated. Nelson MacDonald took part in the attack and remembered seeing Brigadier Hill leading the charge. "He looked like God!" Anderson remembered Hill as a "soldier's soldier," an expression often used by battalion members in describing Brigadier Hill.

There was no let-up from a determined enemy. The tension, the sight of death, and the horror of the paratroopers' daily lives are grimly recalled by Dwight Green, platoon sergeant of Number 3 platoon in A Company. His recollection was that the action took place on June 15, but the war diary notes contradict this, saying the incident happened on June 16. His company was deployed in a defensive position in an orchard at Le Mesnil crossroads.

In the early morning hours of 15 June, 1944, the enemy launched an attack on the "A" Coy. position. The attack was preceded by an extensive mortar and artillery barrage. Self-propelled guns, tanks and infantry spearheaded the attack. A Mark IV tank appeared into the open field, directly to our front, approximately 100 to 150 yards away. In our position we had a Vickers machine-gun and a PIAT gun for support. The Vickers gun opened up and quickly dispersed the enemy's supporting infantry, who quickly withdrew behind a hedgerow.

Pte. A. C. Johnson, the PIAT gunner, fired two PIAT rounds at the tank and scored direct hits. Because of the heavy armour on the front of the tank and the range involved, the PIAT rounds were ineffective. The tank crew quickly retaliated and opened fire with their devastating 88mm. The first shell scored a direct hit on the PIAT, killing Johnson. On instructions from an officer, the Vickers gun commenced firing at the tank. This was a futile effort as it had absolutely no effect against the tank.

It was at this point that I became directly involved. I moved over to an area where I could observe the tank clearly. I then gave the order to the machine-gunner to "cease firing." My contention being that the machine-gun fire was useless and it gave its position away to the enemy. The officer over-ruled my order and told the gunner to commence firing in the hope that the machine-gun fire might destroy the periscope on the tank. I was kneeling on my right knee and clearly saw the 88mm gun traversing, as though looking for a target. At that moment L/Cpl. G. Boyd, who was occupying a slit trench 10 to 20 ft in front of me, stood up apparently to view the action. The tank fired and the shell exploded very close to Boyd, killing him instantly. Shrapnel from the explosion wounded Lt. R. Mitchell, L/Cpl. R. Glenny, Pte D. Fiorito, Pte M. Bone and myself. I received a shrapnel wound through the left knee.

The explosion plus the wound knocked me over. I attempted to get up but fell over again. I realized I had been hit in the knee area due to my torn battledress and the blood around the wound. Within 3 or 4 minutes I was given medical attention by our own company medics.

On June 17 the 3rd Brigade was relieved by the 5th Parachute Brigade and moved back to the banks of the Orne River, where the paras' big packs had arrived from England. Swimming parties were organized in the river, and the men had a change of clothes, the first since June 4. There was a chance to go to the movies and to tour the invasion beaches at Ouistreham. But even out of the line, they were not far from the sounds of war. The area was frequently shelled, and an enemy plane or two swooped low over their tents in the night. On June 25, it was back to the brickyard.

Shortly, fresh reinforcements arrived from England. Curiously enough they were not men from the 1st Canadian Parachute Training Company, but infantrymen. Apparently the thinking was that the paratroopers were being held in reserve in the event of another airborne operation. There were a number of plans drawn up after the breakout from the beaches in mid-August, but the Allied advance was so swift there was no use for the reserve paras. One trooper who hadn't jumped on D-Day was Jim Gioberti, who was left behind to become a batman for newly arriving parachute officers. Because he missed D-Day, Gioberti always felt that he was excluded by battalion members who made the jump. "I'm haunted by it," he said, "because we don't belong to that exclusive group."

Back in the line they came under artillery shelling once more, and constant sniper fire. Heavy rains made life miserable. As night fell, mosquitoes tormented the men as they crouched in their slit trenches. Some soldiers chain-smoked, hoping the smoke would drive the pesky insects away. It didn't. More patrols were mounted and the probing of the enemy's positions continued. To the west of the paras' position, fierce fighting was going on unabated. By the end of July there were six German armoured divisions in the area. Despite this, the time was almost at hand for the final breakout. Early August saw heavy fighting west of the paratroopers' position on the ridge as the Allies inched forward. The 2nd Canadian Corps had finally taken Falaise by August 17. For the first time since jumping on D-Day, the 1st Canadian Parachute Battalion was on the move, too, sweeping through the Bois de Bavent, the woods that were long the killing ground of the Germans and the Canadians. The woods had been abandoned, but heavily booby-trapped.

On August 18, the 1st Canadian Parachute Battalion was given four bridges to seize on the Dives-sur-Mer Canal near Goustranville. Two hours after launching their attack and after fierce fighting, the Canadians had taken their objectives and, for their actions, won two awards for members of A Company, the Military Cross for Captain J. A. Clancy, and the Military Medal for Acting Sergeant George Green. Repulsed in the first attack, Green organized and led a second assault, killing and capturing more than twenty-five Germans. Although he was severely wounded in the leg, Green dug in around the bridge, refusing to be evacuated until every one of his men who had been wounded was attended to.

For the next week, the Canadians harassed the fleeing Germans in a series of skirmishes. It was about this time that Colonel Bradbrooke left the battalion that had become so much a part of his life, from Fort Benning, Georgia, to Shilo, Manitoba, to Carter Barracks in Bulford, to the water-filled gun-pits and slit trenches of Le Mesnil crossroads. Physically and mentally exhausted, Bradbrooke was appointed to the general staff, and was not with the 1st Canadian Parachute Battalion when it finally stopped its dash through France at the small village of

Everything was always done "on the double." This was a training exercise in England. (PA191137/NATIONAL ARCHIVES OF CANADA)

The 1st Canadian Parachute Battalion's second and third commanding officers, Lieutenant-Colonel G. F. P. Bradbrooke (left) and Major Jeff Nicklin. Bradbrooke led the battalion into Normandy, and Nicklin, who later became a lieutenant-colonel, led his troops into Germany. (PA179151/NATIONAL ARCHIVES OF CANADA)

(opposite) Her Majesty Queen Elizabeth visited Canadian paratroopers shortly before D-Day. She is seen here talking to Major D. Wilkins. On the Queen's left is Brigadier James Hill and behind her is Princess Elizabeth, now Queen Elizabeth II.
(PA193086/NATIONAL ARCHIVES OF CANADA)

Major Fraser Eadie, who later became a lieutenant-colonel, took over command of the 1st Canadian Parachute Battalion after Jeff Nicklin was killed on the Rhineland drop. Eadie, who was remembered as being tough but fair, gave up a promising hockey career to serve in the paratroops.
(PA169240/NATIONAL ARCHIVES OF CANADA)

The legendary Brigadier James Hill, DSO, MC (centre) commanded the 3rd Brigade of the 6th British Airborne Division, to which the 1st Canadian Parachute Battalion was attached. Hill was greatly admired by the Canadians for leading from the front. Note Hill's personal bodyguard in the rear.
(PA162027/NATIONAL ARCHIVES OF CANADA)

The 1st Canadian Parachute Battalion's medical officers at Fort Benning, Georgia, in 1942. They are (left to right) Captain C. F. Hyndman, Captain Colin Brebner, and Lieutenant Robert Begg. Brebner was so seriously wounded on his jump on D-Day that his injuries shortened his career as a surgeon after the war. Note the U. S.-style "jump" boots. (PA193084/NATIONAL ARCHIVES OF CANADA)

The first wounded Canadian paratroopers reach England from Normandy. Casualties were high in the battalion's first combat jump.
(PA140571/NATIONAL ARCHIVES OF CANADA)

Jeff Nicklin, a celebrated football player for the Winnipeg Blue Bombers before the war, was killed leading the Canadian paratroopers on the drop into Germany in March 1945. He is seen here at White City Stadium, London, just before the famous Canadian Army–U. S. Army football game on February 13, 1944. The Canadians won the game with a final score of 16–6.
(CANADIAN FOOTBALL HALL OF FAME AND MUSEUM)

The photograph below, taken shortly before the Canadians boarded their aircraft for the drop into Germany, shows A. C. "Slim" Skalicky (left) and Mark Lockyer. Lockyer was gravely wounded on the battlefield in Normandy and narrowly missed an execution-style death. He survived the war.
(PHOTOGRAPHER UNKNOWN)

(opposite) This photograph was taken at the height of the Canadian paratroopers' jump into Germany on March 24, 1945. The jump marked the beginning of a brilliant campaign that took the Canadians from the Rhine River to the Baltic Sea. (PHOTOGRAPHER UNKNOWN)

Corporal Dan Hartigan said parachute jumping in war was irrevocable. Once out the airplane's door, there was no turning back.

(PA193085/NATIONAL ARCHIVES OF CANADA)

The 1st Canadian Parachute Battalion's popular padre, Doug Candy, seen here in Germany in a captured enemy three-wheeled vehicle. (PA193082/NATIONAL ARCHIVES OF CANADA)

An unidentified Canadian paratrooper greets soldiers of the Red Army at Wismar, Germany. The Soviets tried intimidating the Canadians to give up Wismar, but the paratroopers won the day through tact and a show of resolve.
(PA150930/NATIONAL ARCHIVES OF CANADA)

Three unidentified Canadian paratroopers enjoy a beer in Wismar, Germany, at the end of a six-week, three-hundred-mile campaign. (PA193083/NATIONAL ARCHIVES OF CANADA)

Mon Mauger, south of the historic port of Honfleur. With Nicklin in hospital back home, Major Fraser Eadie took temporary command of this battered band of Canadian paratroopers. Of the 543 officers and men who jumped into France, 367 of them had been killed in action, died of wounds, were listed missing, or had become prisoners of war. It was a staggering number of casualties.

Colin Brebner's story, though, had a happy ending. Treated in various hospitals, he never left the Caen area, and when the breakout from the bridgehead came, he was repatriated. His biggest worry as a prisoner of war was that his wife, Beckie, didn't know that he was alive. "Each night I would concentrate in sending a mental message to her that all was well. I could only maintain the concentration for about five minutes, and I did not know if mental telepathy really worked," Brebner said. Beckie never lost hope her husband was alive.

Those of the battalion who survived the bloody initiation that was Normandy were forever marked. This emotional affinity with the 6th British Airborne Division was extended to all Allied paratroopers who made the historic drop, troopers of the 101st U.S. Airborne Division and the men of the 82nd U.S. Airborne Division, who together held the western flank of the bridgehead; joined together by fate, as in the words of Shakespeare's King Henry the Fifth:

"from this day to the ending of the World,
. . . we in it shall be remembered
. . . we band of brothers."

This fraternity of the living and its confederacy of the dead was poignantly expressed in a scene from the 1962 movie *The Longest Day*. John Wayne, who plays the part of Lieutenant-Colonel Benjamin Vandervoot, enters the town of Ste. Mère-Église to find the bodies of the men who were mistakenly dropped in the town. They had been slaughtered and were still hanging from trees and lamp posts, long after they had been killed. "Those bodies!" Vandervoot yells. "Get 'em down! Get 'em down. Down! I don't want those boys left up there."

The ship carrying the Normandy survivors of the 1st Canadian Parachute Battalion sighted the Isle of Wight at 3:45 P.M. on September 6, and shortly dropped anchor in a bustling and crowded Portsmouth harbour.

For the Canadian paratroopers, their longest day was over as well.

7

A FORCE OF WILL

Paratroopers, as a whole, appear to be somewhat
over-pampered and temperamental prima donnas.
Lieutenant-Colonel L. R. McDonald, Canadian Military Headquarters,
London, October 24, 1944

JEFF NICKLIN WAS DISTURBED BY THE APPEARANCE AND condition of the returning D-Day veterans. Gaunt, exhausted, and in some cases, dispirited, the soldiers were immediately issued passes and travelling warrants for a twelve-day leave, from September 12 to 24. The men had a choice of three destinations by specially arranged trains: Scotland, London, or the Midlands. Brigadier Hill had recommended to the Canadian high command that Nicklin be appointed as the battalion's CO and promoted to the rank of lieutenant-colonel and that Fraser

Eadie be made his 2ic. These recommendations were approved on September 8, 1944. They made an impressive pair. Besides being good friends, both men had been with the Royal Winnipeg Rifles before volunteering for the paratroops, and each man was a superb athlete, Nicklin as a football player, Eadie as a hockey star. Together they set about rebuilding the exhausted battalion. New arrivals were selected to replenish the depleted ranks, and a tough training regime introduced, one that both officers would participate in along with the men, even though Nicklin's own wounds still hadn't properly healed following surgery to remove hundreds of pieces of shrapnel. While the booby-trap blast had not fractured any bones, one persistent wound on the right buttock the "size of a quarter," one medical officer noted, oozed infection six weeks after being hit.

Two days after returning from leave, Nicklin appeared before the battalion's first parade and, as the battalion diary said, "laid down" standing orders. Physical training began the very next day, followed shortly by ten-mile forced marches, more street fighting, and a mass jump by the entire battalion on October 9.

It was soon apparent that Nicklin was going to impose tough physical training by the sheer force of his will, which was considerable. Nicklin was not only physically imposing, at six-foot-one, and 190 pounds, his very demeanour was forceful. He was born December 10, 1914, in Fort William, at the Lakehead. His family named him Jevon Albert, but Nicklin was never particularly fond of the name and insisted on being called "Jeff."

Nicklin was only nineteen when he became a member of the Winnipeg Rugby Club and just twenty-one when he played his first Grey Cup game in 1935, when the Winnipeg Blue Bombers became the first western team to win the national championship by defeating the Hamilton Tigers eighteen to twelve. Nicklin played two positions, flying wing and end. Reg Threlfall, the coach, remembers Nicklin being "as good as they come, and one of the better-developed Canadian football players. He was an exceptionally good blocker and simply dynamite when going after passes. Jeff developed faster than most of the local boys. He had mature judgement and when things weren't going just right during a game, I could always find out from him what was wrong. It didn't matter to him if we were down fifteen points with only five minutes to play. He still thought we could win and played that way."

Colonel Bradbrooke thought highly of Nicklin as his 2ic and considered him a friend and a "fine figure of a man." He said there was never "any instance of Jeff not being liked among the officers." This was most certainly true. William Jenkins, while admitting being biased in favour of his co, said he was "my example of an almost perfect co; tough, very tough, but he would not ask anything of anybody that he would not do himself. Perhaps he was somewhat stubborn at times, but he was determined to build, at any cost, a really tough battalion."

Whether all officers endeared themselves to Nicklin is not entirely clear. Madden remembered Nicklin punishing officers who tried sneaking out of the two-mile morning runs by turning them over to the regimental sergeant-major for punishment drill on the parade square, much to the delight of the men.

Bob Firlotte, a junior officer, found himself and four others in front of the mess at seven o'clock one morning, waiting to go for a run after being found in bed by Nicklin.

The colonel arrived in an old Winnipeg Blue Bomber sweat suit and away we went. Now I had spent almost two-and-a-half years in England early in the war as an NCO, during which I competed in track-and-field all summer and cross-country running most of the winter. I stayed behind the colonel for a time and could see that he was breathing heavily and labouring somewhat. At this point, and not realizing the possible repercussions, I pulled up beside him and forced the pace just a bit at first and then quite a lot more. The colonel didn't say a word and stuck right with me, while all the others fell farther and farther behind. When we got back to the mess both the colonel and I were perspiring profusely. Just then it suddenly dawned on me that I was in for a tongue lashing for being so foolhardy. However, the colonel simply turned to me with a smile and said, "That's enough for you, Firlotte. I'll have the others out again, they appear to need it." Well, you can just imagine how popular I was with my peers over that little caper.

With the enlisted men, Nicklin "had that Dutch uncle manner," said Madden. When he was the commanding officer and had men up before him on charge, those who didn't know him were deceived by his manner. They thought they were going to get off. He'd listen sympathetically, then impose twenty-eight days of detention. "March him out, sergeant!"

Those who were sentenced to twenty-eight days wound up at the Field Punishment Camp at Leatherhead, in Surrey, where everything was done at the double. Offenders slept in unheated tents on wooden beds with no mattresses, and only one blanket. Each inmate was assessed on a point system. If they toed the line they could get promoted to a hut with a large stove. "Talking was not allowed while eating, and the food, which was eaten out of mess tins, was lousy," remembered Pete Braidwood, who was sent there by Nicklin for being absent without leave (AWOL) for a day and a half. Braidwood joked he was sent to the cooler for the unpardonable sin of not being a Winnipeg Blue Bomber fan.

Nevertheless, Madden respected Nicklin, finding him fair, firm, and determined. When Nicklin took over, Madden said, he thought discipline was slack and imposed what the men regarded as "chicken-shit" rules. One was that when the men went to the canteen at night, they had to wear boots, rather than soft fatigue shoes. Another rule was they couldn't go out with jackets undone at the collar, even if it was just to the canteen. Hardly Draconian measures, but the men went on a hunger strike.

The protest began October 20, 1944, and soon the press was on to the story, with the army moving fast to defuse a potentially serious situation. Colonel W. G. Abel, at Canadian Military Head-quarters, pleaded with Rear Admiral G. P. Thomson, chief press censor at the Ministry of Information, to clamp a lid on the story. The press censor argued that, while the story was perhaps con-trary to public interest, he was not persuaded to rule that it was contrary to security. This was an important distinction since editors could only be requested, not legally compelled, to suppress a story if contrary only to public interest. To this Abel retorted that the "hunger strike amounted to mutiny and it would be valuable for the enemy to know that a Canadian formation was not at present battle worthy because of incipient mutiny."

The battalion diary notes "great confusion when the men refused to eat. The complaint lay not in the food, but in the treatment of the men by the commanding officer." The weather may have contributed to the bad mood. For five days before the strike, there were heavy rains and wind without let-up. On Friday, October 20, approximately eighty men attended the meal parade but refused to eat. By the following night the protest had spread to everyone in the battalion, and even to the ranks of the training company. By Saturday afternoon, the press had sniffed out the story and the news editor of the *London Daily Mail* called Brigadier Hill, who happened to be acting divisional commander that weekend.

"We hear you have a battalion on hunger strike," the editor said. "Could we come down and look into it?"

Hill said, "Look, there is a war on. The war has to be won.

Give me until Monday and if that strike isn't settled on Monday you can come and see me and look into it."

The paper agreed.

Before lunch on Sunday, Hill ordered the entire battalion into the drill hall, dismissing all the officers and senior NCOS. The regimental sergeant-major (RSM) called the battalion to attention, and in strode Hill to talk to the men. At first, Hill allowed one or two protesters to speak for a few minutes, then took the floor. He told them they were letting Canada down and were acting "like bloody shits." Hill told them there was a more important task, and their petty grievances paled in comparison. Hitler's terrorism had to be destroyed, the Nazis eliminated. If they weren't up to it, he'd replace them. Immediately. "I'm making it absolutely clear. I am giving you an order to go back and eat your lunch." The RSM called them to attention. Hill stalked out. After lunch, a message came to him that everyone had eaten.

Ironically, the hunger strike came only a month after the 1st British Airborne Division was annihilated at Arnhem. Any sympathy that there might have been for the Canadians was certainly dissipated by the news of such high casualties. More than 1,200 were dead, and hundreds captured. The two U.S. airborne divisions that took part lost 3,500 men. Part of the failure could be blamed on one of the German generals, General Student, Germany's premier parachute commander. In any case, the Canadians' complaints were dwarfed by the appalling casualty lists from Holland.

An investigation into the strike was conducted and a report sent to the Canadian high commissioner, Vincent Massey. There were in truth a number of reasons, other than Jeff Nicklin's rules, for the low morale. Two-thirds of the men in the battalion were new since operations in Normandy. Most of the junior officers were new, too, and had "not grown to know their men as they should." The investigators acknowledged that Brad-brooke was often lax "and the men had been getting away with a lot, though discipline as a whole was not too bad." Nicklin was recognized as an "exceptionally strict disciplinarian and in his enthusiasm had been punishing minor offences on a much too severe basis and in some respects had produced regulations, particularly concerning dress within the camp area, which were not entirely reasonable ones."

A few ringleaders were identified who had staged a similar hunger strike earlier in the year, at Camp Shilo, a protest that centred around ill feeling between "para boys" and the NRMA personnel, the hated Zombies. Lieutenant-Colonel L. R. McDonald, who composed the report for Canadian Military Headquarters (CMHQ) and the high commissioner, wrote his rather biased line that "paratroopers were over-pampered and temperamental prima donnas." The battalion diary noted that Hill told investigators he had the utmost confidence in Nicklin and believed the incident had "pretty well burnt itself out."

Not quite. Hill and the investigators discussed what to do with the few agitators and ringleaders, but decided it was unwise to exaggerate the importance of the strike by dragging them out and making examples of them. The brass discussed but rejected the idea of rounding up all the troublemakers and putting them in a draft of infantry replacements and shipping them to the front. Although Nicklin would most certainly have liked to have purged his ranks of the upstarts, it was decided not to take action of any kind. The army didn't want to open itself to possible charges of discrimination or, worse, foul play. It seems by the report that the incident may have resulted in a slight easing up on Nicklin's part, but this is not clear and after fifty-odd years, no one can remember.

The day after the strike was settled, six Canadian paratroopers appeared in Brigadier Hill's office asking to meet with him. They had come to apologize. Hill remembers, "I accepted their apologies and thanked them. Of course I always loved those Canadians and that made me love them more. . . . That couldn't have happened to any other battalion except a Canadian battalion. It was wonderful. The reason I had a grip on them to some extent was that I loved them, literally. If you love people you are commanding and leading, they always reciprocate. They were most receptive in every sort of way. . . ." Brigadier Hill believes the men were ringleaders, but this may not be the case. Others remember the delegation was an ad hoc one comprising men who were embarrassed that the agitators had shown the battalion in a bad light as a result of the protest.

Whether the petty annoyances were lifted, no one can remember. The level of training certainly was not, and by all appearances the tempo quickened. There were battle drills, more street-fighting training, anti-tank training for the PIAT platoon, and a twenty-mile forced march for cooks and bottle washers in Headquarters Company. By the end of the month the battalion had participated in Exercise Eve, another mass jump. From the time the first stick left the aircraft until the last, only seven minutes had expired. The exhausting pace of training was rewarded with a ten-day leave at the end of November. Anyone who had seen them after Normandy and who saw the Canadians now, in their neatly pressed battledress rig, maroon berets, and Canadian jump wings, marvelled at the transformation and the handiwork of Nicklin and Eadie.

As 1944 ended, the Canadian paratroopers looked forward to Christmas and leave. There was a feeling of accomplishment and pride. They had earned a break. Field Marshal von Rundstedt, however, thought differently.

8

FROM THE ARDENNES TO HOLLAND

Looking back on the whole Ardennes involvement,
one would have to say that it was not one of the highlights
of the battalion history in the war. My recollection at this
point, is that the Ardennes was not so much covered
with glory, as extreme hardship, and mystery.

Sergeant R. F. "Andy" Anderson, B Company, 1st Canadian Parachute Battalion

THE PRESS CALLED IT "THE BATTLE OF THE BULGE," BUT THE official name was the Battle of the Ardennes. This short, violent struggle was the last gasp of a desperate German army, played out in a dreadful landscape that tested the will and the resolve of the Canadian paratroopers who were rushed in to help stop the enemy advance.

The Ardennes is the high plateau that links Germany's Eifel region to Luxembourg in the east, and Belgium in the west. This front was lightly defended, the Allies reasoning that its short, narrow, tree-covered valleys and few roads made it far from an ideal position from which to launch a campaign. Besides, the weather was almost always awful; the region is often clouded in fog and subject to sudden storms in summer and heavy snowfalls in winter. Yet, it was from here that Hitler launched his offensive with the aim of retaking Antwerp, the port so vital to supplying the Allied armies. At the same time, Hitler hoped to drive a wedge of armour between the Americans and the British.

On December 16, 1944, behind an opening artillery barrage, the first of twenty-four divisions Hitler had mustered smashed into the Ardennes. Initially the German momentum was impressive, part of their success a result of foggy conditions that kept the Allied air forces grounded. It was a tenuous few days until reinforcements began pouring in to confront the enemy. The two famous U.S. airborne divisions, the 82nd under command of "Slim Jim" Gavin, and the 101st, the "Screaming Eagles," commanded by Maxwell D. Taylor, were thrown immediately into the fray. It was the 101st that went head to head with the Germans at the town of Bastogne, where the struggle was eventually won. Part of the reinforcements included the 1st Canadian Parachute Battalion.

Word reached Carter Barracks on December 23 that all leave passes were cancelled. The troops were told that Field Marshal Montgomery, appointed by Eisenhower to defend and counter-attack in the northern sector of the front, decided the quickest way to stop the German advance was to drop in the 6th British Airborne Division. He would have ordered this launched except the weather over the Ardennes offered zero visibility. On Christmas Eve, the battalion boarded a ship at Folkestone for the brief hop across to Ostende, which was a voyage of great discomfort. By mid-Channel, hundreds of the men were seasick, fouling the heads and the ship's companionways. Boxing Day found the battalion holed up in the small auditorium of a school in the Belgian town of Rumes, waiting for orders. As they were expecting to be moving out momentarily, some members of B Company began priming hand grenades and loading weapons. Suddenly, disaster struck. Andy Anderson, Number 4 platoon sergeant, who started keeping a diary after arriving in Belgium, wrote:

> While standing at the top end of the room, I recall hearing the distinctive "ping" of a striker hitting a grenade primer, and the handle flying. At the same time, I heard Sergeant Hill, in charge of No. 5 Section, call "grenade." I think I yelled to get down, or something, but I do recall throwing myself on the floor, at the side of the stage, then in three seconds, the 36 grenade went off, throwing up clouds of plaster, dust, and, of course, fragments of the casing. Getting up quickly, I found I had escaped cuts. This is the second experience for me with this kind of accident, only I recalled that the last time, I did get an "ass" full of shrapnel, which the nurses in base hospital had fun pulling out of me.
>
> As the dust settled, and my wits returned, I first heard the cry of the wounded and, with some help, I discovered that Sergeant Hill was the worst hit. He lost an eye, probably for the reason that he stood next to the grenade, with a hand over part of his face, which did not protect him. About six other men are wounded, but none fatally, but all had to be hospitalized with fragments.
>
> The Medics and half the company came to see what the commotion was, but in retrospect, it is truly remarkable that half of the platoon were not killed outright. In the midst of all this confusion we moved out, boarded trucks, obviously to take a place in the line somewhere, again we have no hard information.

The grenade accident was a sad note on which to go into battle, the beginning of a month of hardship and deprivation. Moreover, most of the men felt they were never properly informed of their situation. As Anderson noted:

> We can only guess that some discussion is taking place at a higher level, on where we are to go and in what specific role. In this situation all kinds of rumours are flying. It becomes difficult to "keep the lid" on everything.
>
> The only "hard" information is that our division is holding a line against advancing armour who will try to cross the last barrier at Namur, which would then give the Germans a clear run to Paris. This, to say the least, is not heart-warming news. We are essentially shock troops, lightly equipped and armed, hardly in a position to stop massed armour attack. It has been impressed on us that our orders are to stand and fight at all costs. It is a "do-or-die" effort, and we can't count on any support that we know of.

The assault on the town of Roy promised to be a difficult one. While parts of the battalion came under a heavy mortar barrage before the attack, when the Canadians stormed the town they discovered the Germans had skipped out. If the enemy eluded them, the weather did not. The frozen ground made it virtually impossible to dig slit trenches and gun pits. Frustrated, the men tried digging holes by using explosives. It became apparent, too, that they were not really equipped with the proper clothing to withstand the below-zero temperatures and high winds. To keep their feet from freezing, they wrapped burlap sacking around their boots, giving the battalion the look of fleeing refugees rather than a unit of soldiers as they dug into snowbanks for protection from the elements. Anderson noted, "The men are hungry, cold and frozen, and for my part, moving around from section to section has been a painful experience. My one foot is frozen for sure but I dare not remove the boot and wrapping."

Somehow the men persevered. The worst place to be was in one of the forward listening posts. To reach one at night required taking a bearing by compass because of the blowing, blinding snow. In short order, morale began to slip. One night Anderson heard a shot in their own lines and went to investigate. He discovered that a man had shot himself — accidentally, he told the sergeant — while cleaning his rifle. Anderson didn't buy the story. It wasn't plausible that a man would be cleaning his rifle at three o'clock in the morning.

Adding to the miserable field conditions, the Canadians discovered they had an atrocity on their hands when they took over the town of Bande. The Canadians found the bodies of thirty-seven old men, women, and children in the cellar of a bombed-out garage. Fraser Eadie recalled: "The German armoured troops had been in the area and had been chased out but had come back again. They took every male in the village and threw them into the basement of the house and threw grenades in and then shot them up." Anderson's diary noted: "To see young children blown apart in this way for no apparent reason is something not easily forgotten."

Brigadier Hill was outraged when told of the atrocity. He ordered that one man from each platoon in each company be brought to the garage and witness the removal of the mutilated bodies and the highly emotional scene of family and relatives identifying the corpses. The troops were told that the slaughter was the work of the SS and the 14th Panzer Grenadiers. "I think the inference was that we were to remember these units for the future," said Anderson. Jeff Nicklin and Fraser Eadie had watched the scene together. After the bodies were taken away, Nicklin turned to his friend and said, "I am not going to be worrying too much about a lot of prisoners from here on."

In contrast to this scene, and adding to the irrationality of war, was the holding of a brigade sports meet the next day, which featured toboggan races and wood-chopping contests. Hill gave out prizes, and everyone was served tea and cakes. The innocent sports gathering seemed simply one more bizarre episode in a campaign where the enemy maintained a ghostly presence.

Typical of the strain and frustration of the Ardennes operation was this entry from January 17, 1945, in Anderson's diary.

I have been ordered to take out a patrol tonight, a fighting patrol of thirty men, and I have the pick of who I want with me. Our task will be to exit through our perimeter in one direction, make contact with the enemy in the next little town about four miles distant, determine if it is defended, and by how many. We are to fight if discovered, bring back prisoners, and return through another part of our lines just before first light.

We set out at 0300 hours, faces blackened, all loose gear either removed or tied down, main equipment is weapons and grenades. We pass through the lines of No. 6 Platoon who have been alerted to us, then it is a matter of taking cover and following the map route of the railway line, and ditches, and at about 0440 hours, we are at the edge of a small town. It is dead quiet. I split the group in half, working the rear yards, both sides of the street. We only have about thirty minutes to work. On re-assembling, I find that the town is very lightly defended. No contact is made, but German troops have been observed in the houses and in the trenches protecting the area. Rather than get into a fight for a prisoner, I could see time running out, so I made some sketch notes, then started back to our lines.

Getting back to our own lines is far more difficult than I anticipated, since I have been directed to follow a different route on the return that will take us through British lines. After stumbling around in the dark, and with dawn approaching, we finally stumbled into a British outpost, and a nervous challenge; we were let through and back to our own area.

The men are all exhausted, more from continuous nervous tension than the crawling and walking around. In any case everyone hit the sack about 0600 hours, right after having a little food and the traditional shot of rum, which is given to all patrols on return.

Three days later, the battalion learned it was being moved to Holland on January 22. Ironically, as they departed the Ardennes, the men were issued warmer clothing and winter boots, which Anderson noted would have been a "godsend a few weeks ago." Everybody also got a hot bath. In any case the battalion was happy to leave this God-forsaken corner of Europe.

The battalion was told it was to be located in a rest area in Holland, but it found itself instead dug in along the Maas River by the towns of Buggenum, Nunhem, Roggel, and Haelen, where the battalion headquarters were located in the Aldenghoor castle.

Dick Hilborn was now a major and company commander of Headquarters Company, which consisted of staff and its three heavy-weapons platoons — mortar, machine-gun, and light anti-tank, the so-called PIAT platoon. He remembers the action being mostly at long range, with plenty of machine-gun exchanges, sniper fire, and artillery harassing fire. He recalls: "One had to be careful with daylight movement as it usually attracted unneeded and unwanted enemy fire if observed. Night movement was usually all right as it was unobserved.

Both ourselves and the Germans had both standing patrols and reconnaissance or fighting patrols sent out. These crossed the river by boats. On occasion we had patrols stay on the German side, hidden away for twenty-four hours making observations and notes."

One famous landmark was the bridge the Germans destroyed at Buggenum, where Hilborn said "efforts were made to try to cross via the girders but this was not successful. The Germans had dug-in a machine-gun post near their end of the bridge. Our patrols kept close watch on our end."

Shortly after arriving in Holland, the paratroopers planned to assault the Germans on the other side of the Maas River by charging across the collapsed bridge. First they had to find out if this was possible, and a dangerous two-man patrol was organized. The popular Captain Sam McGowan and Andy Anderson made up this patrol. Equipped with ropes, folding ladders, grappling hooks, and white camouflage smocks to put on when they got to the snowy banks on the other side, the two men set out. In Anderson's words:

Personally, I have had lots of patrols, but this is something else again, and I am nervous as hell. The main comfort to me personally is that Sam McGowan will be with me, and he is the best man I know of to be with in any kind of situation. At about 0200 hours, we had some fine food in the mess with Company Sergeant-Major John Kemp, and several others to see us off. We have rubber shoes for climbing, we are carrying the smocks since the white will show up too starkly in the river, but not on the other side.

We went through our defence position at the bridge, one of our company platoons have this point. Lots of handshaking and good wishes all round. Started across the girders, not too bad on our side, but getting close to mid-river the water is running fast and we are spending too much time looking for foot-holds that will lead to other sections.

After about an hour we finally found a solution to the puzzle, and by climbing and jumping a few feet from girder to girder, we got within fifty feet of the German side. Sam McGowan caught up with me and we agreed to wait fifteen minutes to see if we had been detected, since we have been making some kind of noise.

We started to put on our white smocks. Sam got his on OK, but in getting mine untangled with the ropes, mine fell out of my hands and into the river below. This is a real mess but after a quiet discussion with Sam, we decided to push on. We got to the far side just before dawn, we stayed concealed, and marked a few German positions, especially a mortar set-up, then we decided to head back and mark the route for future use. We have to move fast since we do not want to be spotted on the bridge when daylight comes.

It was a much faster trip back, and I'm afraid we were not as careful about noise. In any case we reached our positions about daylight, and we were greeted, then we walked back to Headquarters for debriefing. We had a hot meal, and a shot of rum. We have shown the marked route, and the "Old Man" is happy as hell and he cannot wait to report to Division.

Getting back to the platoon, and feeling good about himself, Anderson fell asleep exhausted. In the middle of the afternoon, he was jarred awake by the field telephone. It was a message from the CO that, beginning that night, and every night thereafter, it was Anderson's responsibility to take patrols across the bridge, a new group every night until they were stopped or detected by the enemy. For many weeks after the first crossing, patrols gingerly made their way over the girders, until one night the Germans spotted the Canadians and raked the bridge with machine-gun fire. The patrols were abandoned. It was apparent that clearing the German positions from the east side of the Maas would require a major assault. While patrols stopped using the bridge, others continued at different places along the river, crossing it in boats at night.

Equally dangerous were the sniper duels between the Canadians and the Germans. Each company had its own small section of snipers. B Company's Donald "Muscles" Ballinger, a boxer from Hamilton, became so addicted to the sniper war that he holed up for days on the top floor of a farm house "so excited," according to the Anderson diary, "by the whole exercise that he will not come down for meals, or even to wash up." This dedication to duty had an immediate reaction from the enemy. Whenever Ballinger let one go, a fusillade of rifle, machine-gun, and mortar fire came back across the river, much to the annoyance of Ballinger's mates. To make it to the outhouse in the garden usually meant a wild dash amidst exploding bullets.

While hit-and-run skirmishes across the river continued, in Anderson's diary he noted more men were lost by accidental shootings than by enemy action. Fatigue and overconfidence in handling weapons were often the cause. "One day the regimental sergeant-major accidentally shot and killed his batman with a .45 calibre hand gun. On another day, two men were killed in a billet when someone was cleaning and assembling a Sten gun. Investigation showed that the man started the bolt action with a magazine in, and he sprayed the whole room full of his buddies before he stopped."

One of the most tragic accidental deaths had occurred in the

Ardennes, involving Sergeant Bill Kelly from Killaloe, Ontario. Nelson MacDonald passed Kelly coming back from a patrol. "Hi ya, Mac," Kelly greeted him. He was carrying five No. 75 grenades around his neck, and another in his hand. A short time later, MacDonald heard a tremendous explosion. Kelly had apparently slipped on the ice and, in falling, had detonated the explosive in his hand, which set off the others around his neck. "There was nothing left to bury," MacDonald said.

The Canadians noticed a difference from their experience in the Ardennes in how appreciative and friendly the Dutch people were. Many members of the battalion were billeted in Dutch homes with families. Hilborn knew that many of the Dutch were near starvation. Holland was one of the few places the paratroopers were in during the war where they couldn't swap cigarettes for eggs, indeed any food. He discovered a bakery in town, but it was closed down because there was no flour or sugar. So Hilborn arranged to have the bakery supplied with the necessary ingredients and struck a deal with the bakers to supply the flour for baking the bread and buns and then split the results fifty-fifty. This they did. For all the time they were there, the battalion had freshly baked goods and sweet buns, much to their delight.

Hilborn was one of the battalion's very few professionally trained officers. Born and raised in Preston, Ontario, where the family owned a large furniture manufacturing company, Hilborn attended Upper Canada College and Royal Military College, Kingston, leaving in 1939 with his "war certificate." His appointment as co to the heavy-weapons company was appropriate. He had grown up with guns, being an expert marksman and skeet shooter. Besides directing his own company, he was given a company of former Dutch resistance fighters, whom he found to be excellent soldiers, using them to patrol and to fill in the thin spots along the battalion front.

There was little relief from the day-to-day sniping and machine-gun duels, but the officers and men were granted overnight passes to go on leave to Brussels. The city was a stark contrast to life on the banks of the Maas River. The bars and saloons were doing a brisk trade and there was a booming black market operating in the open. Anderson noted the locals selling everything from silk stockings to jeeps at street-corner gatherings. He was once offered a truckload of gas. His visit ended on a sad note when he ran into his old buddies from the engineers, whom he had left to volunteer for the paratroops. To his dismay he discovered that half his former squadron mates had been killed during the break-out from the Normandy bridgehead. Anderson couldn't help thinking how ironic it was that, when he'd left the engineers, all his friends had said he was crazy for "joining a suicide unit." Here he was alive, and they were dead.

Rumours were circulating during the middle of February 1945 that the 1st Canadian Parachute Battalion was going to be pulled out of the line and returned to England to prepare for another parachute operation. For once a rumour was true. On February 26, the battalion arrived back at Carter Barracks, Bulford. There, the Canadians picked up their back pay, put on clean uniforms, and took off on leave. Andy Anderson wrote in his diary:

> It has been made no secret that on return from leave, we will begin training at a heavy and grinding schedule to prepare for a major offensive that will mean a parachute drop into the Continent, possibly into Germany. The best guess is that it will be a major crossing of the Rhine since this is the last German line. We are all very certain that our battalion will have a major role in whatever is selected.

On that note, Anderson was right. With Normandy, the Ardennes, and Holland now part of their battlefield experience, the 1st Canadian Parachute Battalion was to play a major role in the vanguard preceding the long-awaited assault across the Rhine River. In less than a month, the battalion was once again fighting for its life.

9
THE RHINE DROP

*If by any chance you should happen to meet one of
these Huns in person, you will treat him, gentlemen,
with extreme disfavour.*
*Brigadier James Hill, DSO, MC, 3rd Brigade, 6th British Airborne Division,
addressing all NCOs on the eve of the drop into Germany*

IN A CURIOUS WAY THE SILENCE THAT DESCENDED ON WESEL in the aftermath of the fire storm of bombs was more ominous than the RAF raids themselves; silence bespoke unseen calamities. Wasn't there always a lull before a storm? In preparation for the Rhine crossing into Germany, the RAF had literally flattened Wesel, a German army garrison town on the east bank of the Rhine. The only building to survive the bombing was St. Willibrord church, standing stark and alone amidst hundreds of moonscape-like craters.

Like most civilians, nineteen-year-old Maria Terwelp and her family fled Wesel after their home was destroyed. Maria's father, who was a schoolteacher, moved his family to Bergerfürth, a small village a short distance from Wesel, where other displaced families and students had also gone. The Terwelp family found accommodation on the Wienhuysen farm and settled down. Only the Rhine River separated the Terwelps from the advancing Allies. They knew it was only a matter of time before they too became a part of the war.

Little did the townspeople of Wesel, Bergerfürth, and Hamminkeln know that this area had been selected as the centre of the greatest airborne operation in history. "For one day," mused Johann Nitrowski, an Hamminkeln historian, "this town was famous, then forgotten." The operation was named "Varsity."

The 6th British Airborne Division was given its objectives on February 25, 1945, by Major-General Matthew B. Ridgeway, who commanded the XVIII U.S. Corps (Airborne). The 6th British Airborne Division, along with the 17th American Airborne Division and the First Allied Airborne Army, would drop in an area barely six miles long and five miles wide to destroy German guns and troops who were dug in facing the line of advance of the Allied land armies, now poised to assault the east banks of the Rhine River. Brigadier Hill's 3rd Brigade, consisting of the British 8th and 9th battalions and the 1st Canadian Parachute Battalion, was assigned to knock out numerous gun-pits, fortified farms, and the village of Bergerfürth, and to take the high ground south of it, a ridge called "Schnepfenberg."

The drop zone assigned to the Canadians of the 3rd Brigade was small, measuring just eight hundred yards by one thousand yards. The biggest concern for everyone, whether landing by parachute or by glider, was the presence of enemy flak and machine-guns dug in around the DZ. Aerial reconnaissance was able to pinpoint any number of heavy or medium flak guns, but it was harder to identify light and heavy machine-gun nests in the aerial photos. A week before Operation Varsity was launched, the Allied planners had identified 712 light ack-ack guns and 114 heavy ones. Moreover, the British and Canadian troops faced a variety of German units, including parachutists, who were being used as infantry troops and only a month before had given a good account of themselves in fighting on the west bank of the Rhine. But for the most part, the German defenders were from various divisions and groups that had been rushed in at the last minute to make a stand. These included one battalion of the 6th Infantry Regiment and one battalion of the 46th Infantry Regiment, both with the 30th Infantry Division. There were another four thousand men with the 84th Infantry Division.

One enemy soldier facing the Canadians was twenty-one-year-old Lance Corporal Reinhard Behrend, who with other wounded soldiers from the western front formed the German Grenadier Division of Great Hamburg (Volksgrenadierdivision Gross-Hamburg). On March 9, Behrend arrived in the area of Bergerfürth and the nearby Diersfordter Forest. "We relieved the Volkssturm units, armed trench workers," he remembered. "Consequently we only had two weeks to familiarize ourselves with local conditions. During the day we could not allow ourselves to be seen because the air superiority of the Allies was overwhelming." This was certainly true. Nothing moved in daylight. To do so was to court death. The Spitfires, Hurricanes, and Typhoons roamed the skies like avenging angels, attacking and strafing at will. As far back as October, one pilot, Bill Olmsted, flying with the famous 126 RCAF Spitfire Wing, described this air advantage. "At zero feet we skimmed over the woods of Germany, along tree-lined roads, by peaceful farms and over minute villages without seeing a solitary person. Other than thin wisps of smoke seeping upward from isolated dwellings, there was no sign of life, although we were nearly one hundred miles behind enemy lines."

By March 1945, even if the low-flying reconnaissance planes couldn't always detect the enemy digging in along the east bank of the Rhine, Allied planners knew he was there in force. With Normandy and Arnhem behind the Allies, the Rhine drop would not repeat the tragic mistakes of either of those campaigns. Inexperienced pilots and navigation errors caused by darkness were all blamed for dropping the Canadians over a wide area in Normandy. While Arnhem was a daylight operation, paratroopers were dropped too far from their objectives and, most important, too far from supporting infantry and artillery. Although the 1st British Airborne Division had made a gallant stand at Arnhem, it was virtually annihilated waiting for armour and infantry to come to its support. These were bloody and costly lessons. The Rhine was to be different.

These paratroopers were to be dropped just a few miles ahead of the Allied land force as it was landing on the eastern shore of the river and in sufficient numbers to overrun the enemy. While Normandy and Arnhem saw paratroopers and glider troops arriving over a one- to two-day time period, this force of fourteen thousand men would descend on the German positions in one fell swoop, with every one of the parachutists on the ground in less than ten minutes, a fearful display of might that would simply overwhelm the enemy. Moreover, the German positions would be pulverized by one of the biggest artillery bombardments of the Second World War, one that would start almost seven hours before the paratroopers leaped from the sky and gliders banked to land on the landing zones.

This air armada, the largest the world had ever seen, was made up of ten thousand aircraft, fighters, and bombers, which would blast and strafe the enemy; C-46s and the newer C-47s to carry the parachute battalions; and various "tug" aircraft pulling more than one thousand gliders.

On March 20, 1945, the 1st Canadian Parachute Battalion left Carter Barracks for a day-long lorry ride to Hill Hall transit camp in East Anglia, where they were briefed behind barbed-wire fences for the next three days. Security seemed even tighter here than before the jump into Normandy. Every garbage truck going in or out of the camp was searched, phone calls were forbidden, and all mail was censored. Although there was no hot water for the first day, Hill Hall camp was comfortable. The men were billeted in Nissen huts and there was even a camp movie theatre, used during the day to brief the men on their objectives. There were maps, photo enlargements, and a plasticine model. The paratroopers were informed in the most minute detail of their missions from brigade down to company, platoon, and section.

Andy Anderson wrote in his diary:

Not only are we in the picture of the total operation, but at platoon and section level. We have studied aerial photos and table topo-photography of terrain of our smallest objective. One cannot escape from the impression that the planners of this operation have learned from past mistakes, and a supreme effort is being made to bring this operation off with maximum efficiency and the least confusion.

Briefly, the objectives were these: the 8th Battalion was assigned the task of clearing and securing the drop zone and clearing out the enemy in the northern portion of the Diersfordter Forest; the 9th Battalion was to march on and seize the so-called Schnepfenberg feature, the high ground south of the

Diersfordter Forest; and the 1st Canadian Parachute Battalion was to attack and seize the Hingendahlshof (a farm) on the western edge of the drop zone and to attack and hold the little village of Bergerfürth south of the drop zone.

Two days before the battalion was scheduled to jump, Brigadier Hill addressed the Canadian battalion's NCOs in a speech delivered with such gusto and exuberance that he was cheered and applauded.

> Gentlemen, the artillery and air support is fantastic. And if you're worried about the kind of reception you'll get, just put yourself in the place of the enemy. Beaten and demoralized, pounded by our artillery and bombers, what would you think, gentlemen, if you saw a horde of ferocious bloodthirsty paratroopers, bristling with weapons, cascading down upon you from the skies? And you needn't think, just because you hear a few bullets flying about, that some miserable Hun is shooting at you. That is merely a form of egotism. But if by any chance you should happen to meet one of these Huns, you will treat him, gentlemen, with extreme disfavour.

Nearly all the NCOs who heard the pep talk remember it vividly because of Hill's confidence and enthusiasm. When he delivered his line that the air support and artillery was "fantastic," his audience burst into applause and cheers in a self-imposed fit of comic relief because they knew the drop was going to be like jumping into a blast furnace.

The next day the battalion was trucked out to the airfield at nearby Chipping Ongar to fit parachutes and to stow everything aboard their assigned aircraft. "Most of the men are cracking jokes, while at the same time checking equipment, ammo, grenades, and small arms," wrote Anderson. As he watched the men in his own platoon it suddenly occurred to Anderson that perhaps 50 per cent of this group had not seen action in Normandy, and another 20 per cent had not joined the battalion until after the Ardennes. Later, Anderson wrote in the diary:

> One reassuring factor and a comfort to me is that I have complete confidence in the leadership and experience of the section sergeants, and every man I am convinced is in top mental and physical form. If ever a fighting unit was ready for anything, that had to be it. My personal concern is that I can measure up and not let anyone down.

The next morning, Saturday, March 24, 1945, reveille was sounded at 2:00 A.M. The paratroopers had been ordered to bed the night before at 8:00 P.M. For most it was a restless and fitful night. After a big breakfast, a meal that was going to have to last them most of the day, and that was for some their last meal ever, the paras climbed aboard the lorries and headed for the aerodrome. Dawn was just breaking as the Canadians swung onto the airfield, looking for their assigned aircraft, roaring by endless lines of silent Dakotas and ungainly glider planes. At the sight of the massed armada, "nerves started to toughen," observed Anderson. "Looking at the faces of the men, everyone is very deep in his own thoughts."

Anderson was to be second man out the door after Captain Sam McGowan, CO of B Company, a Winnipeger much admired and respected by his men for his combat savvy and quick mind. As they lined up alongside the airplane, a jeep roared up and came to a stop. Out jumped McGowan's predecessor, Major Clayton Fuller, who had been until recently B Company's commanding officer. He was being left behind. Those who shook his hand saw his eyes filled with tears. Jeff Nicklin had grounded Fuller. "His five-year ticket came up and the poor guy really didn't know what to do," recalled Fraser Eadie. "But, Jeff Nicklin sorted him out. He said, 'Look, you are going home. You've had enough.' He was busting his backside to go, but Nick said, 'No bloody way.' So that was it, and he just left Fuller behind the wire in the transit camp."

The battalion's new padre, Honorary Captain Doug Candy, was jumping into combat for the first time. The press came to call him "the jumping padre." Candy, much loved by the men, was of slight build, weighing no more than 140 pounds, with an easy smile and twinkling eyes. He said he didn't join the army or volunteer for the paratroopers for any patriotic reason; rather, he felt the men needed to be ministered to. The Rhine jump was to be only his eighth parachute jump. The Anglican priest, of course, carried no gun, but did wear his "dog collar" for the occasion.

As the clock ticked away to take-off time, the men fidgeted with equipment, and made lame jokes. Fraser Eadie remembers:

> Upon arrival at each aircraft the troopers retrieved their equipment and parachute, which had been fitted the day before, and proceeded to dress. Each trooper wore his battle dress over which he wore his parachute jacket, or smock as it was referred to, with its many pockets bulging with personal effects. The crotch piece was buttoned front and rear to prevent the smock from riding up while on the drop.
>
> Over these items of clothing, he placed his web equipment, entrenching tool over his butt, small pack on his chest, ammunition pouches on each side of the small pack. The toggle rope was generally worn around the waist. Bandoliers of spare ammunition for the rifles and Bren guns were slung around his neck in any fashion he desired.
>
> Over this he wore his jump jacket, a sleeveless garment also with a crotch piece. This jacket was to prevent

his parachute rigging lines from becoming entangled in his battle gear. On his leg was strapped a kit bag with a quick release mechanism and twelve feet of rope tied by one end to his parachute harness. [This rope attached to the kit bag has been described to the author at various lengths. Some ex-paratroopers thought it was twenty feet long.] In some cases, the rifle was carried in the kit bag, but more frequently the soldier's personal weapon was carried in his hands.

I elaborate on this to give you a picture of the trooper, because of the scene on the edge of the runway just before enplaning.

Approximately forty minutes prior to take off, the enplaning officer passes the word down the line of air-craft, "Thirty minutes to enplaning." At this sound, nature seems to take over. Despite the complications of remov-ing the equipment so laboriously put on a short time prior, a steady line of paratroopers made it to the side of the runways to indeed remove their gear and do what they had to do.

I daresay that more pages of army message pads were used in those few short minutes than were used for offi-cial purposes for the balance of hostilities.

In the midst of all this, some entrepreneur from one of the companies went down the line enquiring if any-body wanted to buy a good watch. Several alternatives were shouted for the actions he could take with his watch.

Len Hellerud was left a little unnerved himself when the pilot of the C-47 assigned to him lined up the Canadians in groups of five and began taking their pictures and their families' addresses back in Canada. When one of the men asked why he wanted the addresses, the pilot replied, "There won't be any of you guys who will make it back and I'll forward the photos and a letter telling them this was taken before you parachuted into action."

Anderson worried about being flown into action by American crews. "Our previous experience has told us that the Americans are great for food and company but, as for navigation and target, many of us would have preferred to be going RAF, who always seemed to be more disciplined and conscious of the total effort."

It was light now as the pilots kicked over the engines and revved up before throttling back and stepping off the brakes. One after another, the planes lumbered down the taxi-ways, and turned onto the runway. Pushing the throttles to full thrust, the pilots steered for the sky, a scene repeated all over eastern and southern England as thousands and thousands of aircraft climbed out of the circuit and pointed their noses towards Germany.

At the Wienhuysen farm on that Saturday morning in March, the Terwelp family huddled together as the barrage preceding the assault shook the earth like jelly. After daylight, the fighters and the bombers ranged over the countryside, bombing and strafing mercilessly. By dawn Wesel had been captured — what was left of it — and two American divisions were on the east bank of the river. The colossal bombardment had left the enemy along the river banks stunned. At Wesel, British commandos captured a map revealing every German flak position. This information was relayed back to the artillery, who began pounding all the areas around the DZs and LZs.

In the air, the huge airborne armada slowly droned on. Dan Hartigan, who had been promoted to sergeant from corporal after D-Day, and forever the keen observer, later wrote of the flight.

Having come inland from the coast at about 1,200 feet I looked down to see a strange countryside. What I saw wasn't just a western European winter landscape, but ravaged terrain. The vegetation cover was so sparse and looked a somewhat burgundy tinge, mud oozing through turf. I'd never seen anything like it. It was quite surreal.

For a few miles along the flight path and stretching towards the French coast on the Channel, as far as the eye could see, were hundreds of thousands of crater rings. There were so many it appeared almost incomprehensible. Yet there they were, sullen on the surface of this ravaged landscape. We had heard of no heavy artillery attacks in this area, certainly nothing of this concentration of fury.

Then it dawned on us quietly that we were flying over the World War I battlefields. It was a sobering sight, which filled us with melancholy for the suffering which must have gone on down there. Yet here we were less than 30 years later going to fight the same enemy. It took some time to come back to reality.

Shortly before the giant sky train arrived over the DZs, the big guns fell silent, a silence that bewildered the Terwelp family. This was the first time in hours that the ground had not shaken, windows and doors rattled, or the air filled with continuous, rolling thunder. Where they had been rendered senseless by the artillery, they were now stunned by the silence.

Flying in tight formation, the first of the 540 American Dakotas carrying 12 parachute battalions, followed by 1,300 gliders, appeared in the distance nearing the Rhine. In 27 of those aircraft, sitting poised for battle were the men of the 1st Canadian Parachute Battalion. They flew in 3 sections of 9 aircraft each.

In Andy Anderson's plane, someone looking out a porthole shouted, "The Rhine below!" It was 9:55 A.M. Anderson's diary entry reads:

> Looking out of the window briefly my impression was of a very wide lake. I have no idea what I expected, but the river was massive, cold, and uninviting. That's all I remember because within seconds someone hollered out the customary, "Stand up! Hook up!" The navigator opened his door and said, "Three minutes to the DZ." The body of the plane was disciplined confusion, much shuffling, dragging equipment forward, check safety pins in the static lines, count off, then stand in the door, then follows a blast of air. Capt. Sam [McGowan] is leaning out, so I have a good view of the ground. Green light on, 1000 hours on the nose on top of the DZ. I am conscious of other aircraft in the vicinity, also "firecracker" sounds coming from below, plus puffs of smoke. More pushing, close right up, kit bags in hand. Then Green on! GO! GO! GO!

Fraser Eadie was in the first plane in the second group of nine and Jeff Nicklin was in the first plane in the first group. A minute and a half after Nicklin went out the door, Eadie's plane arrived over the DZ. He could see the drop zone ahead, partially obscured by dust and smoke. A few hundred feet above the drop zone, the air was sparkling and the sun was brilliant. It was a beautiful spring day. The 2ic's batman, Private Del Parlee, tapped Eadie on the shoulder, and said, "Looks like a nice day out there, wish I'd gone fishing."

"What a wonderful alternative it would have been, but it was too late to even consider it," Eadie said, with a laugh, years later. Then the green light was on, and Fraser Eadie jumped from the door to let fate take its course.

There are conflicting reports as to how successful the actual drop was. The battalion's war diary said the Canadians were "widely spread" over the area due to the high speed of the aircraft crossing the DZ, implying that the American pilots did not throttle back as they should have. When the Canadians arrived on the drop zone, "flak was fairly heavy," the diary noted. Worse, there was severe machine-gun and sniper fire from at least three sides of the DZ. Brigadier Hill contradicts the Canadian diary. "I asked them [the Americans] to drop the 3rd Parachute Brigade consisting of 2,200 fighting men in a clearing one thousand by eight hundred yards in a heavily wooded area held by the German parachute troops. The drop took six minutes to conclude and was dead on target."

The accuracy of the drop was confirmed by Lieutenant-Colonel George Hewetson, CO of the 8th Battalion, and makes one wonder why the Canadian war diary is contradictory. "The formation used by the American pilots gave a very concentrated drop, and very few sticks, except where there had been a hold-up in the aircraft, dropped away from the DZ," said Hewetson.

Eadie said he landed exactly where he wanted to, but had jumped "from a height most of us later felt must have been around 600 and 700 feet. We had hoped to exit at around 450 feet." It seemed a long time as he drifted down, long enough for a German marksman to get a bead on him. Two rounds snapped by his head with a loud "crack . . . crack." When this happened Eadie slumped in his harness as if he had been hit, going limp with his tommy-gun dangling from his hand. Just before hitting the ground he "came back to life" to make a proper landing.

What Eadie saw as he clamoured out of his harness was nothing short of bedlam. He was obviously caught in triple crossfire from different locations of the drop zone, especially from a clump of trees that came to be known as the "axe-handle" or the "axe-head" since the shape of these woods resembled an axe and its handle. From the west side of the trees, German gunners in pits raked the drop zone, as did others along the northern edge of the axe-handle. In the middle of the DZ was a lone copse of trees from which more machine-gun fire was coming. Eadie felt the bullets whizzing by as he burrowed between the furrows of this freshly ploughed field. Sensing an ever so brief lull, Eadie leaped up, fired two bursts from his tommy-gun at the axe-handle, and took off towards the rendezvous spot. The two-hundred-yard dash seemed to take forever. His equipment felt like a ton as he scooted across the soft earth.

About half-way to the edge of the DZ, Eadie came upon one of three army cameramen who had joined the battalion to record the drop. This was most certainly Mike Lattion, who was shooting black-and-white film on his hand-wound 35mm Bell and Howell cine-camera. He had been hit by shrapnel and was "pretty banged up" and later described the jump and the fighting as "nerve-shattering." Eadie rushed past Lattion and remembers thinking, "He'd best bag his ass out of there if any of us were to see his movies when this particular shambles was over."

Andy Anderson's descent into battle was equally chaotic. It seemed to him to take forever to get down as the bullets whizzed by him. He looked up at the canopy to see two large holes suddenly appear in the silk. He was convinced later that he was told to jump at six hundred or seven hundred feet rather than four hundred. From the air he saw three men dashing across the drop zone heading for the rendezvous locations. He saw, too, bodies of other paratroopers lying in the ploughed field, the parachutes tugging at their dead bodies. Above him, Anderson saw more paratroopers leaping into action and at least one, perhaps two, aircraft on fire plunging towards the earth below.

One of the aircraft was carrying Len Hellerud, whose pilot was going to send those "last" photos back to Canada.

> As we were approaching the drop zone, we were hit in the right engine and tail section, killing the American sergeant jump master who wore a flak suit. The plane was on fire and losing altitude fast. Number one jumper pushed the sergeant out the door and I saw his 'chute open. The green light came on and out we went. I was second last man in the stick, and we were about 250 feet from the ground dead centre of the drop zone. On the way down I was able to see the plane hit the ground and burst into flames with no chances of the crew surviving. It is funny how fate turns around. I'm sure that all the paratroopers returned and none of the flight crew made it to send our photos home.

The plane probably was the same one that Nelson MacDonald saw hit the deck in a fiery explosion. He was mesmerized by the flaming planes and the noise of battle below his swaying feet. He saw a paratrooper fifty yards or so ahead of him suddenly slump in his harness, and go limp, obviously hit.

James Ballingall jumped and landed safely but felt an overwhelming urge to relieve himself. "The first thing I had to do was fire my Sten gun with one hand while kneeling to have a leak," an act that gave new meaning to the expression "savoir-faire."

The arrival of the second wave of Canadian paratroopers eased the situation for the 8th Battalion, who were charged with clearing and securing the drop zone. Temporarily interrupted by the arrival of more paratroopers, the German defenders turned their guns skyward, only to find themselves being raked by paratroopers already on the ground. The fiercest fire-fights took place in and around the axe-handle. An account of the action, written shortly after the war by members of the 224 Parachute Field Ambulance, described the fighting: "The Germans were deeply entrenched all-round the woods, and besides a large number of machine-guns, they were equipped with two field guns cleverly camouflaged to blend with the sand earth and fir trees. The wounded lying out in the open were under constant fire as they tried to crawl to shelter."

There were two extraordinary displays of heroism that day involving the 224 medical unit. In the first instance, two medics trying to reach a wounded paratrooper on the drop zone were fatally wounded before they could get to the man. Corporal Fred Topham, a medical orderly with the 1st Canadian Parachute Battalion, dashed onto the drop zone, and reached the wounded trooper. Despite having been hit himself, Topham dressed the man's wounds, heaved him over his shoulder, and brought him to safety, all the while under constant enemy fire. Topham returned to the drop zone again and again, retrieving more wounded men, all the while refusing to be evacuated himself for painful wounds. Later he dashed towards a Bren-gun carrier that had received a direct hit, which seriously injured three soldiers. One by one he brought them to safety for first aid. His remarkable action won Topham the Commonwealth's highest award for bravery, the Victoria Cross.

Another incredible demonstration of bravery was given by a second Canadian, Corporal John Chambers of the Vickers platoon. The Germans had zeroed in on a crashed glider, and began picking off the survivors as they attempted to flee the wreck. The Vickers platoon called for the mortar platoon to lay down a smoke screen in the hopes of dashing out to rescue the men in the glider. After ten minutes there was still no smoke, and the wounded glidermen were being hit again and again. At this point, Chambers leapt up and sprinted towards the glider, being knocked down twice on the way. Still, he was able to reach the wounded men. In trying to cover the glider with a smoke grenade, Chambers found himself in deeper trouble. The grenade hit a wing of the glider and rolled back at him, drenching him in molten phosphorous. The men in the Vickers platoon watched in horror as Chambers tried neutralizing the phosphorous by scooping earth over his head and face. One paratrooper who couldn't take it anymore, Charlie Clarke, jumped up and raced towards the wounded Chambers. He was also hit, went down, got up, and made it to the glider. About this time, the mortar platoon was able to drop smoke around the stricken men. More paratroopers then rushed out under cover of the smoke and pulled everyone back. Chambers recovered, but Charlie Clarke died of his wounds.

Many men sustained injuries that day. Among the wounded was John Hanson, who broke his collarbone on the jump. Sam McGowan suffered a head wound that caused so much blood he couldn't see. Fraser Eadie came upon McGowan and was startled to see there was a hole in the front of his helmet and one at the back.

"Are you all right?" Eadie asked.

"I've got a bit of a headache," McGowan replied.

"For Christ's sake, Sammy, did it go through?"

In fact, what had happened was the round entered the front of the helmet and followed the liner around to the back before spending itself.

The saddest news was the word that Jeff Nicklin was missing and, later, that he had been killed. It was Lieutenant Bill Jenkins who may have first found Nicklin. "I went into the woods and found Jeff Nicklin hanging in a tree." The scene was a terrible shock that left Jenkins "sick" with sadness. Nicklin had come down in a small copse of trees just north of the axe-handle and directly on top of a German machine-gun nest. When the DZ was cleared of snipers and safe enough, Dick Hilborn led a party of men to the copse to cut down their commanding officer. They discovered that Nicklin's body had been riddled with bullets in the abdomen and groin. The safety catch was still on his tommy-gun and the soles of his jump boots were immaculately clean. His battle dress trousers bore a crisp crease.

There are rumours that Jeff Nicklin had either been "accidentally shot" or "accidentally shot on purpose," for having been a tough commanding officer. Bill Bright, who was from Winnipeg and went on to become a radio personality in Toronto, said he first heard the rumour in the "late 1940s or early 1950s." Why or how such a rumour persists is troubling. Brigadier Hill himself has heard it. "I did hear it but I have never given any credence to it. To me it is a monstrous suggestion," he said. The author even heard the rumour in the hallways of the Directorate of History at the Department of National Defence in Ottawa, that some kind of report or inquiry had been held, a suggestion that James Hill said was ridiculous. "There was certainly no inquiry while they were in England. It couldn't have happened without my knowledge, couldn't conceivably have happened. No. Absolutely none. I think there is far more likelihood in the other stories that went around that a lot of chaps were so bloody annoyed about him being shot up in the trees that they really went for those Germans and they didn't take any prisoners. I would say that would be nearer the truth."

To Fraser Eadie the mere suggestion that this rumour be given any currency dishonours the good name of the battlion. He said:

Let me make it abundantly clear. Nicklin was shot while in the air. Period. He certainly was too experienced a jumper to have allowed himself to drift into the small copse on the DZ. He was obviously heading for the area he and I agreed upon before leaving England. When his body was brought into the battalion headquarters area, where all our KIAS (killed in action) were being interred in temporary graves, I asked Captain Pat Costigan to check the body and report to me with respect to the number of rounds that killed him. Costigan advised me later that it appeared he received five rounds, all entering from a sharp angle below, indicating he was hit by ground fire while still airborne. My own experience confirmed much ground fire at the paratroops as does Andy Anderson.

In all the author's researches in the National Archives of Canada and at the Public Records Office in the United Kingdom, there was no documentation found to support such a rumour, one that must finally be laid to rest, having no foundation in fact. Moreover, having walked the Rhineland drop zone and knowing of the intensity of the fighting, it is ludicrous in the extreme to think an assassin was about his work that day without regard for his own survival.

One problem the Canadians had not counted on was the overwhelming numbers of prisoners who had to be dealt with. The 6th British Airborne Division had taken four thousand German prisoners in two days. As for the Canadian battalion, the war diary noted: "Battalion prisoners constituted quite a problem because they numbered almost the strength of the battalion. It was fortunate that Germans were killed by the hundreds, otherwise it would have been impossible to corral and guard them in the early hours of the operation."

Among the prisoners were Maria Terwelp and her family, who were kept with wounded German prisoners. They were rounded up from Wienhuysen farm, where they had watched the Canadian paratroopers dropping from the sky like so many locusts.

We merely saw the explosions of grenades and the many parachutes in the sky. We heard the deafening gun battle. Then the soldiers with machine-guns stood before us. I was very afraid of the threatening gestures. The soldiers limited themselves to the words, "Hands high. Come on. Let's go. Faster, faster." And in German, "Schnell, schnell" (which they pronounced "sneller, sneller"). First of all they urged us onto the Kellewald estate on the other side of the street. There, in the small and badly destroyed house we were detained with the imprisoned German soldiers. A German soldier was seriously wounded and cried out with pain. No one helped or was able to help. He then died. Later, we had to go through the woods toward the centre of Bergerfürth. From the other side of the street there was still shooting by German soldiers. We heard the shots whistle. We were rounded up with other civilians in the Geerts' garden. We then had to stay with other civilians in the cellar for a few weeks.

Someone else who was captured was Reinhard Behrend. He had fallen in with a group of German paratroopers as it approached Bergerfürth from the west. As they neared where the Canadians had dug in, a German officer ordered his paras to start firing. The Canadians returned the fire, killing, Behrend thought, about forty Germans. He was wounded and carried to the church in Bergerfürth, where there were so many wounded lying around inside that he was placed outside the church. "We were cared for there by both German and Canadian doctors and first-aid attendants. The church forecourt was also over-crowded with the injured. There we got tetanus shots and injections of morphine for the great pain. I suffered a shot to the stomach, to the thigh, and lower leg. Canadian first-aid attendants lit up cigarettes for the wounded and placed them in our mouths to smoke. Our decorations and watches, as well as our rings were taken. That wasn't good!" Behrend was evacuated the next day to Ghent in Belgium, where he was operated on and given massive transfusions of blood, which he said saved his life.

One Canadian paratrooper was less fortunate. He had come down near the edge of the DZ by a farm, getting hung up in a tree. A woman rushed out from the house carrying a pitchfork, which she used to stab the trooper to death. This was the only report of a civilian challenging the invaders, although Captain J. A. Clancy had an unsettling experience after being captured. Dropped four miles northeast of the DZ he was quickly overcome by German soldiers, interrogated, and hauled away.

> During our period of capture we found . . . the German, be he soldier or civilian, incapable of fulfilling a given promise, whether to aid the wounded or give only a drink of water. The civilians regarded us with a mixture of fear, hatred and insolence. One occasion at Nienburg a woman of approximately 50 years of age, stood on the corner as we marched by and spat at us in the column and called us "Schweinhund." Many rear line soldiers and civilians tacitly admitted their lost cause, but afraid of terrorism they continued their part.

Reinhard Behrend admitted the German soldier near the end of the war had few choices. "Germany had lost the war already after her defeat in Stalingrad. We could not avoid serving in the war because we would have been accused of undermining military strength and condemned to death. Similarly, we as soldiers were not able to break rank because then also we would have been condemned to death for cowardice in the face of the enemy. For us young men it was a vicious circle."

Four chaplains made the Rhine jump, but only two survived.

Padre Doug Candy had more than his hands full after the drop. He prayed with the dying and helped tend the wounded. Candy's other grim duties included burying the dead and carefully marking the temporary graves, as he did with Jeff Nicklin. It was with great sadness that he conducted the service for Nicklin. He had liked the CO, even though they had had a bit of a run-in. Candy had constructed plywood walls around his jeep back in Bulford. When Nicklin spotted it, he ordered the plywood taken off. "This is not a sedan, Padre," Nicklin said, "It's a jeep. Take that stuff off."

"He [Nicklin] looked at the chaplain as a bit of an odd-ball," Candy said, chuckling. "Someone who wasn't a military person, who didn't have a weapon to clean. He took us with a grain of salt. Nicklin had a warmth about him. When we were relaxed at the bar, he had a very friendly kind of side to him."

As soon as word had spread that Nicklin was missing, Fraser Eadie immediately took over. When it was learned that Nicklin was dead, Eadie became the new CO of the 1st Canadian Parachute Battalion and was promoted to lieutenant-colonel. The men were very much alike — athletic, candid, and committed. Although known to have a short fuse, Eadie easily and quickly forgot past misdemeanours. One trooper remembered him as a CO who knew "when to be on parade and when to be off parade."

Soon after the paratroopers hit the DZ, the first gliders started coming in. Aboard one was another photographer, Charles Richer. He rode in a Hamilcar with only the pilot and copilot. This glider was transporting a Bren-gun carrier and two motorcycles. Richer sat perched in the carrier for the flight, unperturbed that it was packed with jerrycans of gasoline and mortar bombs. He found the flight uneventful, and was rocked to sleep by the swaying motion of the glider as it was pulled through the sky at the end of the long tow rope. The landing was smooth and quiet. That was not the case for many of the gliders. Once cut loose from the tug planes, these gliders were vulnerable to enemy fire.

An after-action report said the glider landings were made difficult by the presence of haze and smoke, and in some cases intense anti-aircraft fire. Ironically, some of the smoke came from the Rhine, where a smoke screen sixty-one miles long had been laid to cover the movement of the Allied land forces as they crossed the river. More smoke came from Wesel, which had taken yet another pounding from the RAF. The glider pilots found that the photograph they had been issued showed only their intended drop zones, but those pilots who got off course needed a photo showing a larger area in which to pick up their bearings. Gliders landed in the wrong place, some were destroyed in the air, some crashed badly on landing, and others were set alight by enemy fire after landing. Fifty per cent of the 1,300 gliders that left England were destroyed, 650 all told. While some of the crews managed to crawl away from the splintered wrecks, their casualties were listed at 40 per cent. "Gliders were crashing everywhere with landing speeds of about 80 mph, and there were further heavy casualties amongst the glider pilots (100 killed) and their passengers. Many were shot up whilst still flying and others caught fire on the ground," said Tony Leake, who had firsthand knowledge, being a medic with the 224 Parachute Field Ambulance. Of the large lumbering Hamilcar gliders, the kind Charles Richer rode to battle in, only twenty-three out of the forty launched arrived safely. Oddly enough the *coup de main* glider parties were most successful, as they had been in Normandy. The glider troops assigned to seize and hold key bridges over the Issel River and those to capture the town of Hamminkeln were all successful.

The biggest failure of Operation Varsity was that, despite heavy bombardment and air strikes on enemy positions by the drop zone, few of these deadly guns were actually knocked out.

"In fact," the report noted after action, "the degree of neutral-ization achieved was not high and many 20mm, 40mm and 88mm guns remained in action all through the landings, taking their toll of gliders both in the air and on the ground." The post-mortem team concluded that in future drops, the only effective way to get these guns was to "drench" the area with paratroopers and take the high losses that were inevitable.

To no one's surprise, most of the casualties came on the drop zone. George Hewetson vividly recalls the scene:

> You can imagine the sight on the DZ. Thousands of para-chutes drifting slowly to the ground and on the ground. Men getting out of their harnesses and opening kit bags with feverish haste, talking to anyone within call about the jump, for at this stage in an operation to have landed safely is to be inoculated with 100 per cent morale. A scene of indescribable chaos, yet rapidly men were moving off to the RVs and within 35 minutes, 85 per cent of the brigade had reported in. Above it all a continuous stream of air-craft flying east, the scream of the 88mm shells, the puffs of smoke in the sky and the long lazy curves of tracer reaching at what looked like a sitting target.

Casualties might have been higher, according to one captured German officer. The enemy knew the flat ploughed field was perfect for a parachute drop and had dug in heavily. When no Allied paras arrived by nine o'clock in the morning, the Germans moved most of their troops down to the Rhine to counter-attack the Allied force crossing the river.

The planes in fiery death dives, careening gliders, tracers, and mortars combined to spell bedlam. To complete this fantastic tableau, clouds of blue and yellow smoke bombs marking the rendezvous areas, drifted through this chaotic scene.

C Company, repeating its Normandy performance, was the first Canadian unit to parachute into Germany. Moving quickly off the DZ, different platoons raced for their objectives, a line of woods, road junctions, and the Hingendahlshof farm. With amazing speed and skill, C Company had taken all of its objectives within half an hour. The rest of the day and night they exchanged rifle, machine-gun, and mortar fire with the Germans as they fled back from the Rhine and through the company's defences.

It was the same for A Company under command of Major Peter Griffin. Its objectives were taken quickly. Moving at what the war diary called a "fast walk," A Company overran the enemy, "who were dealt with immediately," even though their strength was only 70 per cent. An hour and a half after parachuting into Germany, they were dug in around Bergerfürth, but not without a fierce fight to clear a number of houses. The man who led the attack was the indomitable George Green, who had won the Military Medal for his attack on the bridge over the eastern tributary of the river Dives in August 1944. This day he collected the Distinguished Conduct Medal for his bravery. In part the citation reads:

A strong and determined enemy force was holding a group of fortified houses on the edge of the village. The attack was checked and success hung in the balance. In this emergency, under heavy fire, Company Sergeant-Major Green lead a PIAT detachment up to the first house. Having organised covering fire, he led the assault himself onto the house. After capturing it, he then cleared all the remaining houses in succession. The enemy was full of fight but was worsted by the vigour of Company Sergeant-Major Green's attacks. [Green's] quick and determined action was of the greatest value in clearing a dangerous obstacle and restoring the impetus of the advance. His contempt for danger and eagerness to close with the enemy were an inspiration to the men.

No one was surprised that Green got "gonged" again, the expression for being decorated.

B Company was seeing lots of action, too. Andy Anderson's platoon charged their objective, a fortified farm, in a blaze of bullets. "We were off and running, firing wildly from the hip and covered from the Bren gun. We would over-run bunkers, toss grenades into the houses and barns, generally raise hell and take a few prisoners. The whole episode could not have taken 30 minutes."

For the rest of the day and through the night there was sporadic firing and a little artillery shelling from the Germans. For the most part, the 1st Canadian Parachute Battalion had won the day by mid-afternoon, proud of its achievements and relieved to know that it was no longer alone to face the enemy. At three o'clock, reconnaissance units of the 15th Scottish Division rolled through the Canadians' positions, and before daybreak the following day an armoured column of the Scots rumbled through Bergerfürth. It had been a momentous day, one that was never to be forgotten by those who survived.

The ironic thing about battle is that being shot at is an exhilarating experience — more so, joked Winston Churchill, when you manage to survive. Bullets dramatically sharpen the senses, in fact magnify every sense to the point where sound becomes a crescendo, sight supersensitive, smell vivid, and touch acute. Of course, it is adrenaline that pumps and expands the senses. A few people become addicted to this ultimate excitement. In the television news-gathering business, it is not uncommon to see the same crews and reporters covering dangerous assignments, drawn there not only in the pursuit of facts, but also from a sense of having to test one's limit of moral endurance. There was a hint of "passing the test" in an entry from Andy Anderson's diary, and his personal reflection on the profound consequences of combat.

> At the conclusion of the first day, I think it would be a fair comment to suggest that everyone was both exhausted and personally pleased to have survived. Exhaustion came from the effects, not only of the "fighting" but from the tension that has been building for days. This "high" feeling was of course mixed with feelings of personal loss. We had no idea of total dead, but it had been gradually confirmed through the day that many friends were indeed killed.

The casualty lists were staggering. The 1st Canadian Parachute Battalion lost 67 officers and men, killed, wounded, or missing. The 6th British Airborne Division losses amounted to 1,078 either dead or wounded. The entire body count of British, American, and Canadian that one day reached the appalling figure of 2,500 men. The German defenders had in fact inflicted more blows than they had received. Their dead totalled about 1,000. Four thousand German prisoners survived this brief and violent clash.

"The slaughter was the worst I had seen in the whole of the war," said Tony Leake, a medic who went on to earn a medical degree after the war. "It was a tragic loss of so many specialist troops, which could have been avoided by a night drop." Yet, the Rhine drop exceeded the planners' expectations. Colonel George Hewetson wrote:

> Personally, I think that this was the most successful airborne operation ever carried out, and the biggest one in

that two complete airborne divisions were dropped simultaneously. The airborne operation in Normandy on D-Day was a night drop with dispersion over a wide area and 75 per cent of the men were missing for a long time.

At Arnhem the DZ was some way from the objective which was strongly held. Owing to weather conditions the build-up was slow, and consequently the objective although taken by a small force could not be held. Parachute troops are extremely vulnerable on the DZ. There can be no co-ordinated control, weapons cannot safely be used and although morale at this period is at its peak the enemy can take heavy toll. On the Rhine crossing many parachutists landed in trees and were shot by the ground defenders below.

I do believe that the sight of thousands of aircraft coming in has a very great morale effect on the enemy, and unless they are of the calibre of the Japanese they will not be prepared to put up very stiff resistance.

The price to suppress tyranny is high. Brigadier Hill remembered "as we boarded our aircraft, everyone sensed that they were entering a battle which would mark the beginning of the end. And in the words of Lord Brabourne, so cruelly maimed on the same day as our men at Warren Points, 'When attempting any great endeavour, the important thing is to see it through to the end.' This we were determined to do."

Today the old drop zone is neatly farmed, the fields trim with Teutonic attention to detail. The Nicklin copse remains, the trees now taller against the flat Rhineland fields. Yet there was one scene that was sobering, mystical, and unforgettable for those who witnessed it. One paratrooper had been shot as he descended. He landed upside down in a tree, one arm groping for the ground as if to ward off the fall. Everyone who passed was startled by the colour of the dead man's hand, a vivid and brilliant blue.

In due course, Eileen Nicklin received the following telegram:

DEEPLY REGRET INFORM YOU LIEUTENANT COLONEL JEFF ALBERT NICKLIN HAS BEEN OFFICIALLY REPORTED KILLED IN ACTION TWENTYFOURTH MARCH 1945 STOP DELAY IN THIS OFFICIAL REPORT IS DUE TO NATURE OF ACTION IN WHICH COLONEL NICKLIN WAS ENGAGED AND THE LATENESS OF THIS REPORT IS REGRETTED STOP YOU WILL RECEIVE FURTHER DETAILS DIRECT FROM THE UNIT IN THE THEATRE OF WAR

It was signed by the director of army records in Ottawa.

On June 28, 1945, Nicklin's widow received this letter from Defence Headquarters in Ottawa:

Dear Madam:

Information has now been received from the overseas military authorities that your husband, Lieutenant-Colonel Jeff Albert Nicklin, was buried with religious rites in grave 1, row B, plot 1 of a temporary cemetery located at a point approximately five miles north-west of Xanten, Germany.

The grave will have been temporarily marked with a wooden cross for identification purposes and in due course the remains will be reverently exhumed and removed to a recognized military burial ground when the concentration of graves in the area takes place. On this being completed the new location will be advised to you, but for obvious reasons it will likely take place one year before this information is received.

C. L. Laurin, Colonel

Director of Records for Adjutant-General

In August that same year, Mrs. Nicklin received another letter, this one inquiring where to send Jeff Nicklin's personal effects. These included a Luger pistol in a holster, shirts, towels, socks, undershorts, a box of letters, photos and snaps, one doll (wool), package of playing cards, a box of poker chips, a whisk, an insurance policy, one U.S. dollar (souvenir), a French five franc note (souvenir), key ring, keys, and a lock of hair.

On Tuesday, March 27, 1945, Maria Terwelp awakened to silence. Peering outside, there was no sign of the Canadians. The 1st Canadian Parachute Battalion had left Bergerfürth as they had arrived, quickly.

10
DASH TO THE BALTIC

In that enormous silence, tiny and unafraid, comes up along
a winding road the noise of the Crusade.

G. K. Chesterton, Lepanto

THERE IS A PURPOSEFULNESS TO AN ARMY ON THE MARCH, palpably so when the blood is up. Defenders usually know of an approaching attacker. Word of Napoleon's Grande Armée preceded it by some inexplicable telepathy. In the Peninsular War, the sound of the enemy drums, four beats, a roll, two beats, spoke volumes of impending bloodshed. George Custer rode to his fate at the Little Big Horn amidst the trappings of the victor; guidons snapping in the wind, bugles at sundown, while the Yankee cavalryman sat before his white tent and dined on barbecued elk ribs. T. E. Lawrence's gallop down the Wadi Itm to capture Aqaba was vivid and romantic; flying camel hooves and hooded riders in the dust under a yellow sun.

The 1st Canadian Parachute Battalion's march to glory, its brilliant dash to the Baltic Sea, began quietly in the afternoon of March 26, 1945. The war diary noted:

> At 1000 hours that morning orders came for the Canadians to move south-east along the roadside and then skirt the eastern edge of the woods to reach the Brigade assembly area. Remaining there about three hours, the unit at 1500 hours began a long trek across open country to the east following minor roads with frequent change of direction. After crossing the railway line between Wesel and Hamminkeln, the Battalion paused for a meal in a clump of woods and then crossed the upper Issel [River] before finding shelter for the night in barns and houses.

Naturally enough the battalion was feeling good about its quick successes in and around the drop zone as it turned eastward. It was not until much later that the Canadians knew exactly why their assault was so successful. German general Alfred Schlemm, the commander of the First Parachute Army who was interrogated by the British after the war, said he knew that a parachute drop by the Allies was considered inevitable. To counter an airborne assault it was imperative for Schlemm to determine the most probable spot for the Allied troops to be dropped and for the crossing to be made. Schlemm had captured an Allied report analysing the parachute drop at Arnhem. From the document, he learned that Allied views were now against a paratroop landing too far away from the ground troops destined to link up with the paras. By plotting the areas that were topographically suitable for a parachute drop, it was obvious to

Schlemm they would have to be close to the Rhine. He concluded that the most likely area seemed to be in the vicinity of Wesel.

Schlemm reported on his study to his superiors at Army Group H and to Field Marshal von Rundstedt. They disagreed with Schlemm, reasoning the assault would come closer to the area of Emmerich than Wesel, and so ordered him to send a large part of his artillery to the Twenty-Fifth Army. As the interrogators noted, and as subsequent events proved, this was "a miscalculation of some significance." With the opening stages of Operation Varsity successfully completed, the door into Germany had been battered down and the Allies had crossed the threshold, stated historical researchers at Canadian Army Headquarters.

Another consideration facing the Canadians as they embarked on the last crusade of this long and bitter war was exactly how to deal with the enemy, both military and civilian. The 6th British Airborne Division was to be guided by 21 Army Group's policy on relations between Allied occupying forces and German civilians. First, military government was to be established as rapidly as possible to control the civil population, the Nazi party was to be dismantled, and the civil administrations of the areas being overrun were to be reorganized. It seemed apparent that this was not to happen immediately, so military plans rested with troops on the spot.

At the very top of the list of dos and don'ts in dealing with civilians was that there was to be absolutely no fraternization. The only time the Canadians were to speak to German civilians was when issuing orders, the first order being there was to be no movement of civilians. The only persons allowed to move were prisoners of war, and then only to special cages established to hold them. Inhabitants were ordered to remain in their homes and told that disobedience would be punished. If any civilians were deemed to be "deliberately prejudicing military operations," they were to be shot. The advancing Allied soldiers were cautioned to be suspicious of "apparent friendliness" on the part of the Germans. Troops were ordered not to sleep in houses in which any German civilians were present, and told they must remain armed at all times. Looting and violence to civilians were absolutely forbidden. All commanding officers were ordered to impress that all ranks be made to "realize that the good reputation of Canada" was at stake. Any lack of discipline was to be dealt with immediately and severely. Finally, Germans were to be treated at all times with firmness and courtesy. In the capture of Maria Terwelp and her family, this was the case. The nineteen-year-old school girl was suddenly afflicted with an abscessed tooth. A young German doctor extracted the tooth without any painkilling drugs, but it soon became infected. Maria was much relieved when Canadian medics discovered this and offered immediate treatment.

Terwelp did have one unpleasant memory attached to the presence of the Canadian paratroopers. Her father's Leica camera and lenses as well as a Rolleiflex camera were taken from the Terwelp family. She also recalled that "the stamp collection that was so passionately loved by my father and which was built up over decades, was taken." The family was given a handwritten receipt by "an officer but that has not been recognized" by any authorities either in Canada or in Germany following the war.

On the morning of March 27, 1945, the Canadians were back in the thick of fighting. They awoke to a fog and drizzle and had no time for breakfast. Suddenly out of the fog roared a German tank firing wildly as the men dived for cover. The tank was so close that Andy Anderson remembered "seeing the face of the German tank commander before he buttoned up." The tank was driven off and the men continued their advance in a shower of shrapnel that cut down a British warrant officer named Cooper who, ironically, did not need to be with the Canadian paras. He was a physical education instructor with the RAF, but chose to jump and see action with the men he trained and worked with. "I know that he is older than most of us, has a wife and children in England. Just a great little Limey. Now he is lying dead," wrote Anderson in his diary.

The next two days, March 28 and 29, proved to be typical of the pattern of advance that was to carry the battalion across Germany. Objectives were defined, an attack launched, and defensive positions established until the next objective. The town of Lembeck was quickly taken after some guns in nearby woods were knocked out. It was here that the first of long streams of German POWs began appearing, dispirited and bedraggled, and the first of the Volkssturm "home guard" soldiers, who were either very old men or very young teenage soldiers. Some of them were Hitler Youth who, in Nelson MacDonald's memory, were among the most vicious of the enemy and fanatically fought to the death, giving no quarter. Fraser Eadie riled at the suggestion that some of the enemy who the Canadians encountered in their German assault were of poor standards. "Anyone with a gun," Eadie reminded critics, "is a formidable enemy." In Lembeck, the troopers were issued each a pack of peanuts, one chocolate bar, and twenty cigarettes.

On March 30 the Canadian battalion led the 3rd Brigade into battle, transported to the battlelines first by truck, and later on the rear decks of the Churchill tanks of the 6th Guards Armoured Brigade. Their objectives were to take all the bridges over the Dortmund-Ems Canal. They were momentarily stopped by small arms and sniper fire, but it was most effectively taken care of by the tanks, whose guns simply levelled anything that moved. At one point, as they neared the key town of Greven, the paratroopers sped past a burning British reconnaissance vehicle, which had taken a direct hit that killed the crew. The smell of burning flesh was overpowering and sickening to many of the men.

It was on the approach to Greven that one of the battalion's officers was killed, Captain Sam McGowan, of B Company. McGowan was one of the few permanent force soldiers in the paratroop battalion, having come from the ranks of a great infantry regiment, the Princess Patricia's Canadian Light Infantry. He was an officer who cared deeply for the welfare of his men, and they in turn responded to McGowan by giving their very best. He was one of the few married officers in the paratroop battalion. McGowan died an especially horrible death when a grenade on his belt exploded, which literally tore him almost in half while he remained semi-conscious. McGowan died in Andy Anderson's arms. "He was loved by all the men," Anderson said. "I personally felt a great loss, since over the few years that I had known and worked with him, we had done several two-man patrols in Holland, in the Bulge, and in periods of waiting and in darkness, talking quietly, in some danger, that is when you get close to a man. Sam was a great human being." His comrades left Sam McGowan's body by the roadside, marking the spot with a rifle topped with the man's helmet so the burial parties would not miss the corpse.

A Company was assigned the tough job of taking Greven, which it did with surprisingly few casualties. They had taken what they thought was the key bridge across the Dortmund-Ems Canal only to learn that a second and more important bridge was still in enemy hands. This bridge was soon demolished by German engineers, forcing the 3rd Brigade to cross the river by a small footbridge near the Greven railway station.

A and C companies didn't linger in town but advanced to the edge of the canal, digging in for the night. B Company was forced to stop, having run out of ammunition and fuel. Shelling continued all night, with the two companies along the canal taking heavy casualties. At first light, the battalion's quartermaster rolled into town with ammo and hot food. While waiting for orders to move out, the men discovered a German supply depot in a warehouse. The bonanza included guns, food, and boxes of much prized souvenirs, Nazi swastika flags and armbands. The biggest prize of all was a cache of fresh eggs, which the troopers considered better than gold.

With Greven in Canadian hands, the battalion headed for the next town, Ladbergen, which was being defended by a platoon of German infantry who manned two ack-ack guns, two 22mm guns, and one 40mm gun. Most of the defenders were wiped out, although a few prisoners were taken. The battalion was able to brew up a good meal that night in Ladbergen, much to the chagrin of Major Dick Hilborn and several other officers who had lugged boxes of unappetizing field rations all the way across the two bridges of the canal only to find the men eating fried chicken, eggs, vegetables, and preserved fruits. It was also here that men from B Company found themselves sleeping the night in a looted women's clothing store, the exhausted, unshaved paras dozing among women's lingerie, sheer fatigue rendering them oblivious to the bizarre tableau they must have presented. In another town one platoon found itself in an abandoned pub for the night. When a soldier casually tested one of the beer taps, out flowed a golden stream of brew. The platoon was delighted, until the pub was put off limits. The battalion stayed in Ladbergen the next day, where German troops staggered in throughout the afternoon to surrender.

On April 3, in a driving rainstorm, the Canadian paratroopers took off for their next objective, the town of Wissingen. On that day alone, the battalion travelled forty miles, an advance so great that the Canadians were simply overrunning the enemy, who didn't know in most cases where the advancing Canadians were until they found themselves surrounded.

Much of this rapid advance was due to Brigadier Hill's idea of leap-frogging his three battalions towards the dazed enemy. Fraser Eadie recounts a conversation with James Hill, who wanted his "Canadian cavalry" to take one particular town:

"I want you to go down and roust them out of there," Hill said to Eadie.

"What else?" Eadie asked.

"What else do you need?"

"Well," he said, "what kind of support do I get? It's about nine o'clock at night, and it's starting to get dark. What about artillery?"

"Oh, we've outrun the artillery. They are no good to us," Hill said.

"Well, what about the tanks?"

"They can't fight at night," Hill replied.

"I really don't have anybody. It's just us, isn't it?"

"Yes," Hill answered. "What more do you want? Go down there and have them cleaned out by 0400, would you?"

"Oh, sure." Eadie groaned.

"Brigadier Hill was forever volunteering his brigade and we were all very proud of his confidence in us," Eadie recalled.

The 3rd Brigade was on a roll. As it approached the next big town, Minden, the brigade learned that the enemy had evacuated the city. The battalion took over the town, setting up headquarters in the posh Victoria Hotel, the best in town. Many of the paratroopers who took part in the "mad dash" across Germany have vivid memories of the advances. Anderson said his memories are of "running through towns and villages too fast to recollect." When the Canadians were stopped by shooting, "the tanks merely levelled the opposition." He remembered at one town an impatient James Hill rushed up to the lead tank and banged the side with his thumb stick, ordering the tank commander to "bash on!"

And on they bashed. By April 6, the battalion crossed the Weser River, sweeping through Lahde, Wolpinghausen, Luthe, and Ricklingen. Fraser Eadie recalls an incident when he was astonished to see a soldier attacking the enemy while carrying a basket of eggs.

> I said, "For Christ's sake, drop the eggs," and he said, "I can't drop the eggs, it's taken me a long time to get them." All of a sudden the section leader was down and everyone dropped and the guy with the eggs puts his eggs down. We finally got everything cleaned up. Around the corner of a barn came this kid with a mess tin with four eggs in it, and he said, "Would you like some eggs, Colonel?" I said, "You bugger." That kid never wavered going across there. He would drop down and shoot but then get up and pick up his eggs. But those things happened, crazy things happened and I would wonder why anyone would do that. And yet at the time it was damn important that that guy get those eggs up to where he was going because his section would need them when he got there. It was the mind of the Canadian paratrooper that was so vital to everything the battalion did. They thought about one another. They were just a tight knit group of guys.

The number of prisoners created many logistical problems, as did the increasing numbers of civilians the Canadians inherited as they seized one town after another. Everywhere they went, out came the white flags and the phrase "nix Nazi," wrote Anderson in his diary. "They were not to be trusted but we are not in a position to classify anyone by politics. Everyone is an enemy . . . if one wants to stay healthy."

At the town of Brelingen on April 10 there was a disturbing incident. Four German soldiers dressed in civilian clothes were captured. One tried to escape and was severely beaten by the paratroopers. Despite the beating, he tried to escape a second time and was shot dead. His papers showed that he had been a doctor. The surviving prisoners confessed the man had been trying to form a group of German soldiers dressed in civilian clothes to sabotage the Allied advance.

The battalion stayed two nights in Brelingen, where they got a much needed and appreciated bath. If any of the paratroopers was feeling sorry for himself, the mood was dispelled by the sight of a small number of prisoners of war liberated by the Canadians. As they trudged past the barbed-wire cages, the sickly POWs, both men and women, emaciated and dressed in rags, feebly waved at their liberators, tears streaming down their faces. Many of the men tossed the prisoners cigarettes and chocolate bars. The prisoners pulled themselves to attention, saluting the advancing Canadians.

The battalion's advance by the middle of April was less spectacular than the forty-mile-a-day runs back at the beginning of the month. Anderson's diary gives the flavour of the march.

> The advance generally from the 10th to the 17th was a day-to-day struggle, walking partly, sometimes on rear decks of tanks; town after nameless town taken. Men are wounded and killed in isolated rear guard actions, but no major assault is called for. The routine is advance as far as possible by day, dig in for the night and hold. We are making about 15 miles a day rotating with other companies and platoons for the point.
>
> There is a clear feeling that we are away out front somewhere, tired and weary, no supplies have reached us. We are using captured German guns and ammo, and in most

cases using their captured rations, which for the most part are lousy. The rumour has it that we are set to drive the Germans all the way to the Baltic, just where that is at the moment, I am not clear. One thing is emerging, from the prisoners we are taking and units we have overrun, the war seems to be closing fast, as least in our front. In our prisoners, we are running into a conglomerate group, airmen, sailors and young children, trying to fight a group action. Where we run against them, they stay and fight, but it is a far cry from the fanaticism of the Panzer and SS battalions we ran into in Belgium and Normandy.

Prisoners are becoming a headache. We have no facilities, and we can't spare men to guard them or escort them to whatever rear we might have. So we try and keep them with us; they can dig trenches, carry some of the heavy gear, until we find some way to turn them over to another unit. In a quiet moment looking at perhaps 50 prisoners, it suddenly occurs to me that the age is perhaps 15 years, the kids have tears in their eyes. It is hard to convince some of them that they are not being asked to dig graves for themselves. I suspect that our general appearance, the red berets, the camouflage jackets, and the look of our tired men, unshaven, is enough to frighten most people who may have heard stories about the "paratroopers" being ruthless. I can't feel any great hostility against these kids, they show me pictures of family and loved ones, and we try to converse in broken German. Their greatest hope is to see family again.

The day after Anderson wrote the above entry, Captain J. A. Clancy, who had been captured after being dropped beyond the DZ back on March 24, suddenly appeared in the battalion's midst.

With no thought of being repatriated as a prisoner of war, Clancy immediately took over his old command as CO of A Company. His escape had been simple enough. Marching with a column of prisoners towards the Allied lines, Clancy simply walked out of the ranks and started looking for the 1st Canadian Parachute Battalion. He was warmly greeted and welcomed back.

Clancy may well have expressed more than a little surprise at the appearance of his "lost" battalion. After an intensive month of hard campaigning, the Canadian paratroopers looked a sight that could have well inspired Hollywood decades later in creating *The Dirty Dozen* or *Garrison's Guerillas*. Some of the men appeared so outlandish that Brigadier Hill diplomatically asked Lieutenant-Colonel Eadie whether it was quite necessary for his men to adopt such a variety of costumes. Several men were walking around with bowler hats they had "liberated" from a men's store. Another wore a hockey sweater that bore the name "Flin Flon." Others were garbed in German para smocks, similar to their own camouflage Denison smocks, and carrying a variety of captured weapons. Lugers were especially favoured and proudly displayed in waist belts. When the battalion eventually reached Wismar, Eadie himself acquired a beautiful V-8 Horch Auto Union limousine that had been commandeered in the battalion's name by Quartermaster Eddie Friel. Another officer rode around in his own Buick, which he had also "liberated."

Each day grew warmer as they neared the end of April and with each passing mile there were fewer casualties. On April 29, the 1st Canadian Parachute Battalion moved out on foot, headed by six pipers from a Highland unit, and marched to the banks of the Elbe River. This historic river was crossed the following day at mid-afternoon. Ahead lay the city of Wismar and the Baltic Sea. In two days, the Canadians would be bathing in the salty waters of the Baltic. Ahead, too, lay a tense confrontation with the Red Army, a nose-to-nose test of will to determine who was to rule Wismar, Canada or the Soviet Union.

The first night that Canadians bedded down on the east bank of the Elbe turned out to be a nightmare for C Company, which came under heavy artillery fire, not by the Germans but by Americans still on the west bank of the river. It took nearly two hours to get word to the Yanks that they were shelling Canadian positions. The men of C Company were dismayed to find an ammunition train sitting on the tracks in the middle of their positions. Luckily, the train was not hit and, miraculously, there were no casualties.

May 2 dawned cold and foggy. The battalion had planned to advance to the town of Wittenberg, which stood between them and Wismar. Little did the Canadian paratroopers suspect, as they climbed onto the tanks of the Scots Greys and piled into the personnel carriers, that before the day was out triumph would be theirs. Enemy resistance was so slight that the column reached Wittenberg by 9:20 A.M. James Hill sensed resistance was fast crumbling and gambled on a lightning thrust to take the 3rd Brigade all the way to Wismar. Besides, Hill was acting on orders that had come from Winston Churchill.

At Lützow, the armoured column carrying the paratroopers stopped in a wood. Before it stood an amazing sight. Three thousand German soldiers offered to surrender. The battalion war diary captured the remarkable scene:

The confusion was indescribable in that wood. German civilian women, men, and children were there with the troops, and when the troops were lined up three deep on the road, many had their wives and children with them to accompany them on the trek back to prisoner of war cage. This was because the rumour was ripe that the

Russian Army was only nine miles away. The civilians and soldiers were terrified of the Russians and wanted only to be taken by us.

After refuelling the column, Hill ordered it eastward without delay. There was no resistance from the enemy. In fact, the Germans wanted the Allies to advance as far as possible into Germany to stem the flow of the marauding Red Army. "They reasoned that the more territory we occupied," the battalion diary noted, "the less the Russians could occupy."

The scene was bizarre, unbelievable. As the column roared towards the sea at breakneck speed, it flashed past thousands and thousands of German troops lining the roads and crowded in small villages. In a strange twist of irony that only war can produce, the same enemy that dedicated itself to killing the Canadians only weeks before now stood at the roadside cheering them on.

Major Jerry McFadden had written to his wife, describing this incredible scene.

Yesterday we had one of the most astounding days I have ever experienced. The German army gave up by the thousands. We rode on tanks and in trucks from 5:00 A.M. to 4:00 P.M., sometimes at 40 mph. In a heavily wooded area, at one point, we drove through what looked like a divisional strength tank corps, all lined up facing the road, officers and crews standing at attention, saluting as we drove by. They were out of fuel.

Then to complete a sensational day, I got permission from the CO to go out and contact some Germans who wanted to surrender. Having 'acquired' my own civilian car, I picked up an interpreter and a husky rifleman, put a white flag on the car and started out. Soon we contacted a German officer riding a motorcycle. He spoke English, somewhat, and he wanted to surrender and asked if we would return with him to meet his co. I didn't expect it was so far, more than twenty miles. In a small town, surrounded by German civilians and soldiers, we made arrangements for them to surrender to the British army. Not only did we get 500 soldiers lined up in the town square, but many civilians, and started them en route to Wismar.

Andy Anderson experienced the same eagerness of the enemy to lay down their arms. "It was something out of the Apocalypse," he remembered. "German civilians and soldiers were coming through by the hundreds, fleeing from the advancing Russians."

Jerry McFadden had written home: "All Germans, civilians and soldiers, are terribly afraid of the Russians, and I don't blame them. The Russians are just as tough as they look and can they drink!! The vodka stuff is like 'kick-a-poo joy juice.' ... But I can't blame the Russians, they are just paying back a few scores. Wonderful fighters, even the tank drivers (girls) are tough. We are much too soft."

On reaching Wismar, B Company was ordered to take up positions beyond the railway and astride a main road leading into town. C Company was sent to the eastern edge of town to cover bridges from the eastern approaches. A Company was held in reserve around the marketplace near the battalion head-quarters, which was set up in Frundt's Hotel. All through the afternoon and night, an undulating flow of German refugees and soldiers came through the lines by the thousands. The sit-uation in town became so snarled that everyone was eventually turned towards some fields outside of the city, where they could be processed for POW holding camps.

Another problem that occurred, and one that was unique to the Prussian mind, was that German generals and senior officers made it clear they would surrender only to someone of equal rank. Anderson's men solved the problem with Canadian ingenuity. "This amused our guys who quickly promoted one of the privates to general, who with much solemn formality accepted swords and side arms." One enemy general endured the shame of being ordered by the Canadians to carry his batman's luggage.

In the course of one hour, B Company had collected so many German weapons it soon had a pile of guns ten feet high and twenty-five feet long. When the Canadians began clearing houses to take over as billets, they found even more German soldiers in hiding. Adding to the flowing column of soldiers and refugees there suddenly appeared hundreds of escaped prisoners of war whose only concern was to get to the nearest airfield or seaport for the long-awaited journey to England.

And then the Russians arrived.

At approximately four o'clock in the afternoon, Major Jack Simpson, commanding C Company, encountered a Russian advance party demanding entry into Wismar. The Canadians refused, at which point the Russians became belligerent. It was patently clear they had anticipated with some eagerness the prospect of taking over Wismar, a city ripe for plucking as it had suffered little from war damage. "My first reaction," noted Anderson, "was that they were the hardest bunch of toughs I have ever seen. Their uniforms make no sense; they seem to be peasants, armed with German weapons." Half of the group was drunk. The Russians demanded that the Canadians accompany them back to their own lines, but this offer was wisely refused. Instead, one officer and his driver were escorted into Wismar to confer with the Canadians. "It was quite unofficial," the battalion war diary states, "since he had no idea that we were in Wismar until he came to our barrier [roadblock]. He had come far in advance of his own columns and was quite put out to find us sitting on what was the Russians' ultimate objective."

At Canadian Headquarters, it was decided to send a party back with the Russians to make contact on their lines. Lieutenant Pete Insole, Andy Anderson, Private "Doc" Warnock, and a Private Dyock, who spoke Polish and some Russian, took off with the Russian party, eventually finding themselves being fêted at a full banquet table piled high with caviare and dozens of vodka bottles by a bemedalled general and young Russian women soldiers. The Canadian contingent barely survived the feast to make it back to Wismar, where two of their numbers, Insole and Dyock, immobilized by booze, were carried unconscious to their beds.

The next day, an official liaison was appointed in the figure of Richard Hilborn, whose combat record was equal to the Russians', and whose upbringing in one of Preston, Ontario's, leading families and his education at Upper Canada College and RMC were tailor-made to deal with the Soviets' *bonhomie* and sometimes devious charm. Hilborn measured up to the task at hand, as the war diary attests: "He brought in several distinguished visitors who proved to be the most persistent and thirsty drinkers we had ever met. They could stow away prodigious quantities of the stuff and it was amazing the way they stood up to it . . . until they finally sagged into comas." Fortunately, a wine cellar was discovered in A Company's position. Although it had been looted, there was still enough wine and champagne to keep the Russians happy. Two days later the diary noted again that camaraderie between the Canadians and the Russians continued at "a high pitch, with much drinking and handshaking." Years later, Fraser Eadie said the only reason he agreed to Hilborn's visits was because he had had "a bellyful of undisciplined Russian soldiers. I refused to participate in any social funtions with them."

The billets in Wismar were the best the battalion had found in their sweep across Germany. There were electric lights and radios in all the houses, and for the first time the Canadians were able to listen to BBC reports, which were simply spectacular. More than seventeen thousand German troops in their area had packed it in, and German forces in Italy had also given up. The most stunning news was that Adolf Hitler had killed his mistress, Eva Braun, and then had blown out his brains in the bunker behind the Reich Chancellery in Berlin, where the Red Army was now in full control. One disturbing bit of news was that German forces in Denmark were still holding out, and if they continued to do so, the 6th British Airborne Division, it was rumoured, would be sent to finish them off. This was not to be the case.

There was a festive air about Wismar as the realization set in that the days of killing and being killed had ended. Many of the Canadians, despite the no-looting policy, had in truth "liberated" everything with wheels, from bicycles to German sports cars. The no-fraternization policy was not taken very seriously as many German women had returned to the homes where the paratroopers were billeted and were doing washing, mending clothes, and, in some cases, cooking for the Canadians. The presence of the Russians, on the other hand, was posing any number of problems, beginning with attempts to intimidate the Canadian paratroopers. Again, Anderson's diary offers a lively account of one confrontation that was potentially dangerous. On May 7 he wrote:

> The Russians are becoming more of a problem. They are allowed to pass freely through our lines and roadblock, and even with a better quality soldier than we originally linked up with, they are still entering our lines in a drunken condition. This occurs both day and night and at all hours of the night. The Russians are obviously drawn to the large city which we hold, and while there has been a little pushing

and shoving going on, our orders are to try to keep the lid on the situation, which often means "turning the other cheek." A very difficult pose for our men.

In the early hours of this morning, I was awakened in the headquarters by loud banging on the front door. Someone went to see what the situation was and he immediately discovered three Russian soldiers, who insisted on coming into the house. They were very drunk and somewhat abusive. I had let them in and escorted them to the kitchen area, where by use of sign language we offered coffee to help sober them up. However, they were more interested in our weapons and gear lying around. While I was out of the room for a few minutes, it seems one of our medics agreed to exchange a .45 calibre pistol for one of the standard Russian burb guns, and within a few minutes I heard a shot from the .45 and when I went into the kitchen I found the Russians had accidentally discharged the pistol and the slug had struck one of the medics who was trying to sleep on a mattress on the floor. The slug has torn into the upper thigh, passing through, not breaking any bones.

The shot sobered up the Russians, who were disarmed by the paratroopers and escorted back to their lines. When the incident was reported to battalion headquarters, Anderson was reminded that "orders came from a very high source" that the Canadians were not to treat the Russians harshly, or interfere with them in any way. It was very difficult for Anderson to comprehend the attitude of the Russians, who seemed to him "more like an enemy than an ally."

The following day, May 8, was officially designated VE Day, Victory in Europe Day. After all they had been through, the celebration was anticlimactic. Besides, the booze was starting to dry up and many men spent the day listening to celebrations by shortwave radio coming from London and New York. Still, noted the war diary, there was enough liquor — gin, whisky, vodka, wine, and schnapps — for some to "acquire the inevitable hangover." Heads had cleared three days later when the 3rd Brigade staged a march for Major-General Eric Bols, who had succeeded Richard Gale as commander of the 6th British Airborne Division. It seemed a fitting end to a costly campaign, with the 1st Canadian Parachute Battalion marching with the 8th and 9th battalions with whom they had soldiered so brilliantly. The German population turned out en masse, watching "docilely but sullenly." A few days later, a thanksgiving and memorial service was held in Nikolaikirche in Wismar. Padre Doug Candy led the paratroopers in prayer in memory of their dead comrades who made the supreme sacrifice on the long march to victory.

Then, a new rumour spread through the ranks like a prairie grass fire: the Canadians were going home.

11

HOMECOMING

Halifax has been proud and grateful in the past to
welcome Canada's returning heroes, but never so proud
and grateful as now of the opportunity of saying "welcome
home" to you who have come back to us from the
bloodiest and most merciless war of history.

John E. Ahern, acting mayor of Halifax

I F IT'S TRUE THAT AN ARMY TRAVELS ON ITS STOMACH, IT IS
equally true that it sustains itself by rumour. An avalanche of
rumours inundated the 1st Canadian Parachute Battalion in
the wake of victory in Germany. These baseless reports had the
6th British Airborne Division and its battalions variously
headed for the Far East, India, and even Palestine. Amidst the
speculation as to the destiny of the Canadian paratroopers,
Fraser Eadie learned that Canadian Military Headquarters
wanted the battalion to revert to Canadian control. Very

quickly orders were issued to move the Canadians back to Carter Barracks at Bulford. The last week in Germany was spent leisurely, with sports events and swimming parties on the shores of the Baltic.

On May 20, 1945, the first contingent of paratroopers reached Bulford and the beginning of a nine-day leave. As it turned out, the 6th British Airborne Division was sent to Palestine in what was perhaps the first postwar "police action," a situation that did not sit well with the British paratroopers. This was "a very hard pill to swallow," in Andy Anderson's memory, "when one thinks of troops surviving the war in Europe, only to be killed in some police action in a remote part of the world."

Other than being given leave, the Canadian paratroopers were still in the dark as to their immediate role. It was an unsettling period that wasn't helped any when, half-way through their leaves, word was flashed throughout Britain for members of the 1st Canadian Parachute Battalion to return to their barracks. Anderson was sitting in a movie theatre in Brighton when the order was projected onto the screen. With heavy hearts and thoughts of being shipped to the Middle East, the Canadians arrived back at Bulford. To their delight they discovered that the battalion was going home en masse and would leave in days by train for Scotland to board the *Ile de France.*

As soon as the war ended, the business of repatriating the fighting troops was begun. In fairness for the men and women who had served overseas the longest, a system of points earned for foreign service was devised. Each month's service in Canada counted for two points, overseas service counted for three points per month, and the scores of married men with children were increased by 20 per cent. While some of the paratroopers would have scored high in these categories, if each man was assessed under the point system, it is doubtful that many would have qualified for quick repatriation. In any case, they were on their way home and the last thing on their minds was trying to interpret the bureaucratic thinking of the army brass.

There was a festive air to the departure as the first draft of the Canadians marched from their barracks for the last time to the train that waited to speed them on their way. Flags and bunting snapped in the wind, a band played lustily under a huge parachute badge and a large maple leaf that had been fashioned from sheets of plywood and painted gold. When the officers and men had already boarded the train, they learned that James Hill had personally come to bid "his Canadians" farewell. Then, something extraordinary happened. The Canadians refused to leave until each man had shaken hands and said goodbye to Brigadier Hill. One by one they left the train to salute the man who had led them in battle and to final victory. The last entry of the war diary for the month of May captured the emotional and tearful farewell.

> There was a great deal of handshaking all around, and finally the draft moved out in the train to the accompaniment of the strains of "Auld Lang Syne." It was the end of almost two years' association with the British 6th Airborne Division, and though we felt sad at parting with so many friends, we could look forward to meeting soon our families and friends at home, who had done so much for us.
>
> But in everyone's mind, as we left Bulford, was the thought that many . . . were being left behind, in English fields, in Ranville cemetery, in Normandy, other cemeteries in Belgium, Holland, and latterly, on the Dropping Zone and in other places scattered through Northwest Europe.

At nine o'clock on the evening of June 15, the hum of shipboard life was suddenly broken when a shudder ran through the ship. The *Ile de France* was moving "on its way to the promised land," said the war diary. A rousing cheer went up throughout the ship from everyone aboard. Brigadier Hill recalls their departure:

> I remember thinking as my 1st Canadian Parachute Battalion set sail for Halifax, Canada, in the *Ile de France* at the end of the war, what splendid ambassadors for their great country they had proved to be whilst isolated and serving with the 6th British Airborne Division throughout their war in Europe.
>
> They were called upon and paid the full price for freedom and service to their country: 128 men never returned to Canada; 294 had been carried off the field of battle wounded; 84 had suffered in German prison camps. A casualty list of over 500 men from that one and only battalion.
>
> I thanked the Almighty for the privilege of being their brigade commander.

The trip home was unfortunately marred two days later by the accidental shooting death of one paratrooper by one of his friends with a captured German pistol. An on-board Court of Enquiry cast a cloud of gloom over the remaining passage home.

This incident did not deter a huge welcome-home ceremony staged by the city of Halifax, with festivities that began at ten o'clock in the morning. When the *Ile de France* docked on June 21, Halifax Harbour exploded with train and boat whistles, all giving the V-for-victory signal. Prime Minister Mackenzie King sent his personal greetings, and the acting mayor of Halifax, John Ahern, presented Fraser Eadie with the symbolic key to the city. As the paratroopers formed up to march through the streets of Halifax, a navy band struck up "The Maple Leaf Forever." Along the parade route, office girls threw candies and blew kisses at the passing paras, who then boarded four special trains and departed for the Maritimes, Montreal, Toronto, and western Canada.

The battalion, being the first fighting unit to return from the war, was greeted with exuberance and genuine enthusiasm. All across the country, at different train stations, platform ceremonies were held as reporters and photographers clamoured for interviews and photos, especially of Corporal Fred Topham, who had just been awarded the Victoria Cross for his heroic rescue of wounded paratroopers at the Rhine drop zone. These continuous celebrations reached a climax when the special train reached Toronto's Union Station, where the welcome was tumultuous. The *Toronto Daily Star* captured the spirit of the homecoming with the headline "Canada's Heroic Paratroopers Are Welcomed to Toronto," and an emotionally charged story that read, in part, "Police managed to keep the spectators from the marchers, except in less than a half-dozen cases. 'He's my boy,' cried Mrs. J. F. McLaughlin as she convinced a patrol constable that she should march in the parade beside her son. As the maroon berets of the battalion swung into Yonge Street on the victory march to city hall, wives, sweethearts, relatives and little children rushed into the smartly marching lines to embrace the heroes. One veteran picked up his little girl and carried her to city hall."

Andy Anderson wrote one of the last entries in his personal diary:

This was a once in a lifetime opportunity for all the men of the battalion. Again, it was apparent that we were the first unit intact to return and all the accolades were heaped upon us by the press and politicians. The unit in

many ways was perhaps the ideal formation to be subjected to all the attention, since it did represent all
provinces and it did have the reputation of being the elite
of the army, not to take anything away from many great
infantry units who would arrive home much later. Of
course, it must be admitted that much of the attention
was focused on Fred Topham and his being awarded the
Victoria Cross just a few days earlier, so it added to the
mass hysteria that greeted us!

Everyone was given a thirty-day disembarkation leave until
July 27, when the men reported back to duty to a camp located
at Niagara-on-the-Lake and, once back, joined the queue to be
discharged. While waiting for the paperwork to be completed,
the men relaxed, swam, played baseball, and helped local fruit
farmers harvest their crops. The sight of the young, tanned
paratroopers cheerfully picking peaches was a startling contrast
to their activities just a few short months before.

On September 30, with official orders to disband the 1st
Canadian Parachute Battalion, Fraser Eadie signed the papers
that brought this unique and proud Canadian Army battalion
to its end. As the unit's last member, Eadie then arranged for
his own discharge and, like the tens of thousands of citizen-
soldiers, returned to civilian life to enjoy the peace that had
been won at such tremendous cost and sacrifice.

12
FIFTY YEARS ON

To say it was an honour to have commanded such a force
is indeed an understatement. Only those who had the privilege
of a fighting command can know the everlasting and
deep emotional feeling of satisfaction from having
served alongside such gallant men.

Lieutenant-Colonel G. Fraser Eadie, DSO, CD, commanding officer of the
1st Canadian Parachute Battalion, 1945

WHEN MEMBERS OF THE 1ST CANADIAN PARACHUTE BAT-
talion Association attended the twenty-fifth anniversary of the
Canadian Airborne Regiment at Camp Petawawa in 1993, they
brought with them the same exuberant spirit that they had displayed on the long, fighting trek from Normandy to the shores
of the Baltic Sea. So intent were some members to join the Airborne Regiment's mass jump, that the association president
Andy Anderson thought it was wise to issue an order that under
no circumstances would any of the aging veterans be allowed to

don parachutes to jump with the young regulars. "Don't even ask," the order read.

It was this kind of commitment and sense of adventure that the paratroopers carried with them back into civilian life at war's end. For such a highly motivated group of men, it was not surprising how well they prospered, almost without exception. The paratroopers' roll-call is a long one. The few mentioned here are merely illustrative of their peacetime achievements and successes.

PRIVATE RAY ANDERSON. Brigadier Hill's Metis bodyguard survived his wounds of Normandy, to suit up again for the jump into Germany. The Native warrior and the cultured British soldier met many years later in the Norman fields, where they had found fame. Ray Anderson remained in the army, serving with the Princess Patricia's Light Infantry, and eventually retiring as Master Corporal.

SERGEANT RONALD F. "ANDY" ANDERSON. The strapping six-footer returned to his home town of Toronto, where he joined the police force. In the 1950s he enrolled at Northwestern University in Chicago, where he earned a degree in traffic engineering, later becoming an expert in his field. For years, Anderson was the very popular and tireless president of the 1st Canadian Parachute Battalion Association, retiring from this post only recently.

LIEUTENANT-COLONEL G. F. P. BRADBROOKE. The man who led the Canadian paratroopers into Normandy left the military after the war, living in Canada and England. When he retired, Bradbrooke was residing at Ramsey, the Isle of Man. In corresponding with the author, Bradbrooke had revised his thoughts on the effectiveness of paratroopers. While viable fifty years ago, he opined, "nowadays I cannot help but feel that parachute troops and glider-borne troops would be rather ineffective. With troop-carrying helicopters and with helicopter gunships for protection and support, you can leave parachutes and gliders at home! Troops could bring in heavier armaments, could concentrate on the ground and organize more speedily closer to their objectives. Night attacks would be much more effective. There would not be the necessity for lengthy parachute training."

CAPTAIN COLIN BREBNER. This energetic medical officer, who was so painfully wounded in the D-Day drop, was repatriated after hospitalization in England and returned to medical practice as a surgeon. Regrettably, the wounds he sustained prevented him from continuing to work as a surgeon. The constant pain made it impossible to stand long hours at the operating table. Eventually, he pursued a second career as a medical administrator. He lives in Ottawa.

HONORARY CAPTAIN DOUGLAS CANDY. Doug Candy became a familiar figure on the campus of the University of Toronto in postwar years, where he served as chaplain to returning war vets who went back to school. Having seen more than his share of bloodshed and death, Padre Candy became active after the war in the promotion of world peace, attending one of the first postwar peace conferences in Helsinki, Finland. Although officially retired, he is still working with seniors in his Toronto parish.

LIEUTENANT-COLONEL G. FRASER EADIE, DSO, CD. The battalion's last commanding officer, Fraser Eadie returned to the Ford Motor Company, retiring as an executive after many years of service. He reverted to reserve status, commanding the Winnipeg Light Infantry (Reserve) for a number of years, and was the honorary president of the 1st Canadian Parachute Battalion Association, and a past president and honorary president of the Canadian Airborne Forces Association. From August 1989 to June 1994 he served as colonel of the regiment for the Canadian Airborne Regiment. He is the Canadian trustee for the 6th British Airborne Division Normandy Trust. Colonel Eadie also holds the U.S. Silver Star for gallantry. Following the death of his wife, Colonel Eadie married Eileen Nicklin, widow of Jeff Nicklin who was killed in the Rhine drop. They live in Oakville, Ontario.

SERGEANT-MAJOR GEORGE GREEN, DCM, MM. George Green was born in New Jersey. As a metallurgist before the war, he knew that in the United States he would be prevented from enlisting and instead would be "sent to a plant to measure metal for the duration." He never returned to the United States to live. He married a Canadian and worked his way up the corporate ladder as a sales executive for a regional brewery and for John Labatt Limited. This highly decorated paratrooper retired to North Delta, British Columbia.

MAJOR RICHARD HILBORN, M.I.D. Major Hilborn returned to his home town of Preston, Ontario, and the family's furniture manufacturing business. He also served ten years "on the bench" in Kitchener, Ontario, as a Justice of the Peace. Ironically, Hilborn, who survived the fierce fighting without a scratch, lost a leg after the war when he was accidentally shot by a friend while trap-shooting. He retired to Elora, Ontario, and for many years spent winters in Mexico.

BRIGADIER JAMES HILL, DSO, MC. This greatly respected officer had one final assignment when hostilities ended. He became the military governor of Copenhagen. To everyone's surprise Hill left military life at the end of that duty. Had he chosen to remain in the army, it seems certain he would have reached the highest level of command, given his extraordinary gift for leadership. Instead Hill returned to his family fuel business and a somewhat depleted fleet of ships, due to losses during the war. For a while Hill lived in Montreal, where his family firm opened a Canadian branch of the business, an opportunity that permitted him to renew his friendship with many former members of the Canadian battalion. A charming dinner host and witty after-dinner speaker, Brigadier Hill not long ago addressed the British Staff College. He said: "Gentlemen, looking back on my life I now realize I have three claims to fame. I was the longest-serving fighting brigade commander who never had the sack nor promotion in World War II. I was only the second man in history to have found a cuckoo's egg in a winchat's nest — and those of you with ornithological tendencies will know that was a feat of superb one-upmanship. To my considerable discomfort, I suddenly realized that it was not beyond the bounds of possibility that I might be the most ancient warrior ever to have addressed this august assembly." Brigadier Hill lives modestly but comfortably in a cottage in West Sussex, England, bird-watching and tending to his marvellous garden.

PRIVATE TED KALICKI. The native of Warsaw, New York, never did swear allegiance to the King. He returned to his home town, where he became its longtime mayor. Normandy remains the most memorable event in his life, and "as the history of the battalion shows, proved our worth in the scheme of things."

PRIVATE MARK H. LOCKYER. The man who saw his comrades murdered in cold blood as they lay wounded on the battlefield, went back to the family farm "because I needed a year to get my nerve back." Later, Lockyer helped prepare a regimental history. He forsook life on the farm and was not keen on going back as the lead hand on a dynamite team in the mines. Instead, he enjoyed a successful career in the field of insurance.

PRIVATE NELSON MACDONALD. This bilingual native of Ottawa returned to his home town, and joined the post office. MacDonald, whose harrowing escape from behind enemy lines with John Madden was a story-book tale, served in all three of the battalion's campaigns: Normandy, the Ardennes, and the Rhine drop. He is apparently one of the few para-troopers who has returned to the Ardennes. He went to a conference of international philatelists in Brussels. When the meeting ended, he toured the route the battalion had followed. In one town, when the mayor learned he was a Canadian para-trooper, MacDonald was given the man's bedroom as his guest for the night.

LIEUTENANT JOHN MADDEN, CD AND BAR. One of the few para-troopers to make a career out of the army, John Madden went on to serve in numerous peacekeeping operations from Pales-tine to Laos. After retiring from the Canadian Army in 1974, Madden moved to New Zealand, where, in his fifties, he returned to university and earned a degree in Law. He practiced as a solicitor until 1985, when he "really retired."

LIEUTENANT-COLONEL JEFF NICKLIN, OBE, M.I.D. The memory of this brave officer killed in the Rhine drop is kept alive today with the Jeff Nicklin Memorial Trophy, which is awarded annu-ally to the most outstanding player in the Western Division of the Canadian Football League. The sensational Doug Flutie has won the award the last four years running. The trophy is in the custody of the Canadian Football Hall of Fame and Museum. The main parade square at CFB Petawawa also carries the Nicklin name. Following the end of the war, his remains were disinterred from the temporary grave in Germany and reburied at the Canadian military cemetery at Groesbeek, Holland.

CORPORAL FRED TOPHAM, VC. The battalion's most highly decorated soldier, Fred Topham, remained the model of modesty despite his heroic action during the Rhine drop. He resisted all attempts by civic officials who wanted him to attend official functions as a "home-town boy." A gentle, reserved figure, Topham was respected with great affection by all members of the 1st Canadian Parachute Battalion. He was known simply as "Toppy." Originally from Weston, Ontario, he went on to work for Toronto Hydro.

Despite revisionist thinking, the idea of men cascading through darkened skies, their faces daubed with greasepaint, and armed to the teeth like pirates, is a most romantic one. Who among them can forget the excitement and apprehension of leaping into the unknown, the sound of the parachute exploding open, the slamming of the D rings of the static lines clanking against the fuselage; who can forget the white-hot arcs of tracer fire sizzling across this canvas, the smell of oily gun barrels, of sticky canvas, and the lingering aroma of high octane fuel of the departing C-47s sweetening the night skies?

The paratroop veterans, although on average two years younger than other Second World War Canadian veterans, have eased into their seventies, their memories a kaleidoscope of profound events that are as vivid today as they were fifty years ago. Two generations have come and gone since the end of the greatest war in history. Then, as now, a grateful Canada recognizes what they did was right and just.

Their deeds were their honour.

ACKNOWLEDGEMENTS

WRITING A BOOK IS NOT UNLIKE GOING TO WAR. YOU ARE NEVER quite sure of the final outcome, it always costs more than was anticipated in time and money, and along the way total strangers become friends. This journey was a long one, almost three years. Besides Canada, I travelled to the United States, England, France, and Germany. Everywhere I went I was met with kindness and enthusiasm for the project. I'm indebted to all the paratroop veterans who responded to my queries and questions. I particularly want to thank John Madden, Ted Kalicki, Richard Hilborn, and Mark Lockyer for providing me with insights into the parachute war. I am grateful to Ronald F. "Andy" Anderson, the dedicated president of the 1st Canadian Parachute Battalion Association. Remember, half-way through the research the scandals surfaced involving the Canadian Airborne Regiment. The last person veterans wanted to talk to was a journalist. I also found Mr. Anderson's diaries, kept during the Ardennes campaign and the Rhine drop, to be extremely valuable, as were those of Dr. Colin Brebner, whose night drop on D-Day was a most horrifying experience.

I'm indebted, too, to my wife, Anne Acland, who helped me with the research and correspondence and who soldiered through a bad case of the flu while we were in rainy Normandy. My son, Philip, was also a big help, and his knowledge of Canadian military history and current affairs never ceases to impress me.

For giving weary travellers a place to stay, we thank friends Keith McKewen, Don and Helen Johnston, Neville and Judy Acland, Jorg and Jutta Weiland, Mary and Stewart Guth, and Fred and Beverley Walmsley.

Brigadier James Hill, DSO, MC, and Mrs. Hill were most gracious to Anne and me. I especially thank Brigadier Hill for turning over material from his personal archives and for taking the time to answer my seemingly endless queries. His lovely English garden is something to behold. The battalion's last commanding officer, Lieutenant-Colonel Fraser Eadie, DSO, CD, was most helpful too.

In Germany, Johann Nitrowski and his wife, Marianne, couldn't have been kinder. As an historian, Mr. Nitrowski may just well be the definitive voice on Operation Varsity.

In the United States, Beverly McMaster, reference librarian, and Vivian Dodson, chief librarian, at the Donovan Technical Library, the Infantry School, Fort Benning, Georgia, provided me with useful material. I thank Frank Hanner, curator of the Infantry Museum, also at Benning, and Jodie Eskirt and Denis Lavoie at the Military Museum and Canadian Airborne Forces Museum at CFB Petawawa. At the National Archives of Canada I thank Edwidge Munn and Barbara Wilson, and most especially Paul Marsden, whose scholarship is impressive. I also thank Dr. Ben Greenhouse at the Directorate of History, DND, for his advice. Thanks also to Barry Hyman at the Manitoba Provincial Archives and to Louise Froggett and Elizabeth Dagg at the Canadian Football Hall of Fame. Terry King's researches on my behalf at the Public Records Office, Kew, Richmond, Surrey, were most appreciated. Others who offered a helping hand were Diedre Allan, Charles Howard B. Bradbrooke, Mrs. M. L. Bradbrooke, Gary Boegel, Jeff Keay, Dr. Tony Leake, Dan Nyznik, John Macgillivray, Laurie Monsebraaten, Jack MacLeod, Roxanne M. Merritt, Isobel Ripley, J. N. Scarr,

M. Alice Shepard, Jeff Stelik, and Brigadier-General Denis Whitaker, DSO, CM, ED, CD.

Among the staff of the secretariat at the School of Journalism and Communication, Carleton University, I thank Freda Choueiri, Eleanor Egan, Connie Laplante, and Darlene Zaremba for their help over the years. A special thanks to Tamara MacFadden for her many word processing skills.

I'm happy to be published again by Malcolm Lester, whose counsel is always wise. Thanks also to Anne Shone for impeccable editing.

If I have forgotten someone, I offer sincere apologies. War and writing have one thing in common, fatigue.

BIBLIOGRAPHY

BOOKS AND ARTICLES

[Members of the 224 Parachute Field Ambulance]. *Over the Rhine: A Parachute Field Ambulance in Germany*. Sarafand, Palestine: The Canopy Press, 1946.

Ambrose, Stephen E. *Band of Brothers, E Company, 506th Regiment, 101st Airborne: From Normandy to Hitler's Eagle's Nest*. New York: Simon & Schuster, 1992.

———. *Pegasus Bridge: June 6, 1944*. New York: Simon & Schuster, 1985.

Arthur, Max. *Men of the Red Beret: Airborne Forces 1940–1990*. London: Warner Books, 1992.

Berger, Monty and Brian Jeffrey Street. *Invasions Without Tears: The Story of Canada's Top Scoring Spitfire Wing in Europe During the Second World War*. Toronto: Random House of Canada, 1994.

Chaliand, Gérard. *The Art of War in World History: From Antiquity to the Nuclear Age*. Berkeley: University of California Press, 1994.

Cholewczynkski, George F. *Poles Apart: The Polish Airborne at the Battle of Arnhem*. New York: Sarpedon Publishers Inc., 1993.

Crookenden, Napier, Sir. *Dropzone Normandy: The Story of the American and British Airborne Assault on D-Day 1944*. New York: Charles Scribner's Sons, 1976.

Desquesnes, Remy. "Memorial, 6th June, 1944, Sword Beach, Ouistreham," *Editions Ouest-France* (La Guerche-de-Bretagne), 1990.

Gavin, James M. *Airborne Warfare*. Washington: Infantry Journal Press, 1947.

———. *On to Berlin: Battles of an Airborne Commander 1943–1946*. New York: Viking Press, 1978.

Graham, Dominick. *The Price of Command: A Biography of General Guy Simonds*. Toronto: Stoddart Pub. Co., 1993.

Hartigan, Dan. "The Development of the 1st Canadian Parachute Battalion," *Espirit de Corps*, June 1992.

Hoyt, Edwin P. *Airborne: The History of American Parachute Forces*. New York: Stein and Day, 1979.

Keith, Ronald A. "Sky Troops," *Maclean's*, August 1, 1943.

Macdonald, Charles. *Airborne*. New York: Ballantine Books Inc., 1970.

Maclean, Norman. *Young Men and Fire*. Chicago: University of Chicago Press, 1992.

Madden, J. R. "Ex Coelis," *Canadian Army Journal*, vol. 2, no. 1, January 1957.

Marshall, S. L. A. *Night Drop: The American Airborne Invasion of Normandy*. Boston: Little, Brown, 1962.

Middlebrook, Martin. *Arnhem 1944: The Airborne Battle*. London: Viking, 1994.

Nicholson, G. W. L. "The First Canadian Parachute Battalion in Normandy," *Canadian Army Journal*, vol. 5, no. 8, November 1951.

O'Brien, R. Edward. *With Geronimo Across Europe*. Sweetwater, Tennessee: The 101st Airborne Division Association, 1990.

Plaice, Ellis and McKay, Norman. "Red Berets 1944," *The Illustrated London News* (London), 1994.

Ryan, Cornelius. *A Bridge Too Far*. New York: Simon & Schuster, 1974.

——— . *The Longest Day, June 6, 1944*. New York: Simon & Schuster, 1959.

Saunders, Hilary St. George. *The Red Beret: The Story of the Parachute Regiment at War, 1940–1945*. London: Michael Joseph, 1950.

Shapiro, L. S. B. "How Monty Foxed the Hun," *Maclean's*, May 15, 1945.

Stacey, C. P. *The Canadian Army, 1939–1945: An Official Historical Summary.* Ottawa: King's Printer, 1948.

Taylor, Maxwell D. *Swords and Plowshares.* New York: W. W. Norton, 1972.

Tucker, Ron. *A Teenager's War: The Harrowing World War II Story of a Young Parachute Soldier.* Spellmount, Kent: Spellmount, 1994.

Wheldon, Huw, Sir. *Red Berets into Normandy, 6th Airborne Division's Assault into Normandy, D-Day 1944.* Norwich: Jarrold Publishing, 1982.

Whitaker, W. Denis and Shelagh Whitaker. *Rhineland: The Battle to End the War.* Toronto: Stoddart, 1989.

Wickens, Barbara and Hal Holden. "Coming Down from the Sky," *Maclean's,* June 6, 1944.

Willes, John, assisted by Mark H. Lockyer. *Out of the Clouds: The History of the 1st Canadian Parachute Battalion.* Port Perry, Ont.: Port Perry Printing Limited, 1981.

Zim, Herbert S. *Parachutes.* New York: Harcourt, Brace and Company, 1942.

UNPUBLISHED MANUSCRIPTS AND
DOCUMENTARY COLLECTIONS

Hartigan, Dan. "1st Canadian Parachute Battalion Assault on the Rhine: The Ride, the Drop and the Objectives," 1988.

Hewetson, Lt.-Col. George. "Over the Rhine — Action of 8 Parachute Battalion," a transcript of a walking tour of the 3rd Brigade's Rhine drop zone, 1947.

Leake, R. A. "The History of the 8th Battalion in Normandy, 6th June to September 1944," 1994.

Low, Floyd. "Canadian Airborne Forces, 1942–1978," an essay submitted in partial fulfillment of the requirements of the honours program for the degree of Bachelor of Arts, History, University of Victoria, April 1978.

"Syllabus of Training for Qualification as Jumper," Camp Shilo, Manitoba: The Parachute Training Centre, March 1943. Airborne Museum, CFB Petawawa.

AUDIO:

"Canadian–American Army Rugby Game." A transcript of the broadcast by Capt. Ted Leather. Transmission to Canada February 14, 1944. National Archives of Canada.

"The Pegasus Trail — Historical Walking Tours." Compiled by Lt.-Gen. Sir Michael Gray for Brittany Ferries and the Airborne Assault on Normandy Trust, 1989.

"Temperance and the Total War Effort." Prime Minister W. L. Mackenzie King. Transcript of the broadcast. Ottawa, December 16, 1942. National Archives of Canada.

DIARIES:

Anderson, Ronald F. "The Rhine Diary" and "The 1st Canadian Parachute Battalion in the Ardennes," March 24–May 8, 1945 and December 23, 1944–February 26, 1945.

Brebner, Dr. Colin. "Recollections of a Canadian Parachuting Medical Officer During World War II."

1st Canadian Parachute Battalion. "War Diary," vols. 1–34, August 25, 1942–September 30, 1945.

NATIONAL ARCHIVES OF CANADA:

"Airborne Forces: Future Operations. Employment of Airborne Forces." 21 Army Group. January 19, 1944.

"Airborne Forces: Future Operations." 21 Army Group. August 1944.

"Memorandum on the Requirements for a Continental Airborne Operation." 21 Army Group. September 3, 1943.

"Memorandum to the High Commissioner for Canada — Hunger Strike." Lt.-Col. L. R. McDonald, Canadian Military Headquarters. October 1944.

"Military Government Relation with (German) Civilians." 21 Army Group. March 1945.

"Minutes of Canadian–American Football Committee Meeting, 1400 hours, 17 Cockspur Street, W.W.1 London." 29 December 1943

"Minutes of Meeting at Norfolk House to Discuss Future Policy Relating to the Employment of Airborne Forces." 21 Army Group. 10 August 1943.

"Narrative of First Two Days of Present Operation." Maj. J. A. Clancy, Lt. V. E. Fleming, and Capt. R. E. Harrison. 24–25 March 1945.

"Operation Plunder: The Canadian Participation in the Assault Across the Rhine and the Expansion of the Bridgehead by 2 Canadian Corps." Canadian Army Headquarters Historical Section Report No. 19. 23/24 March–1 April 1945.

"Operation Varsity-Plunder 1 Cdn Para Bn Operational Order No. 1." 21 Army Group. 17 March 1945.

"Overlord: Timing and Weather." 21 Army Group. 14 December 1943.

"Policy on Relations between Allied Occupying Forces and Inhabitants of Germany." 21 Army Group. September 1944.

"Report on Investigation into Death of Lieutenant-Colonel J. A. Nicklin, CO 1 Can Para Bn by Capt. R. A. Virtue, ARCO, 2 Cdn Corps." 7 April 1945.

"Selection of Paratroops at 1 Canadian OCTU Selection Centre." Lt.-Col. J. W. Howard, Canadian Military Headquarters. 1 April 1944.

Public Records Office (Richmond, Surrey, United Kingdom):

6th Airborne Division Intelligence Notes, no. 15, "Organization of a Wehrmachtkommandant," and no. 35, "Estimate of the Enemy Situation of March 17, 1945."

6th Airborne Division Report on Operations in Normandy 5 June–3 September 1944.

6th Airborne Division Report of Operations (Varsity) 24 March–2 May 1945.

INDEX

George V, 44

German senior officers, surrender of, 185-86

Germans: and Allied soldiers, 173-74; and enemy para-troopers, 63; in Republic of Ireland, 46; and sabotage, 180

Gioberti, Costantino "Jim," 19-20, 35, 37, 115

Glenny, L/Cpl. R., 114

gliders, 8-9; on D-Day, 93-94; Rhine drop, 162-63

Gold, Ted, 1, 4

goods, commandeered, 182

Gort, Commander-in-Chief Lord, 44

Graham, Dominick, 45

Grant, Ron, 59

Gray, Lt.-Gen. Sir Michael, 69-70

Greece, airborne attack by Germans, 9

Green, Sgt. Dwight, 18, 50, 55, 82, 89, 113

Green, Sgt.-Maj. George W., 18, 104, 116, 200; Rhine drop, 165-66

grenade accident, 129

Grenadier Division of Great Hamburg (German), 143

Greven, taking of, 175-77

Griffin, Maj. Peter, 106-107, 165

Gulf War, friendly fire, 110

H

Halifax, welcome-home ceremony, 194-95

Hamilton Tigers, 57, 59, 120

Hanson, Capt. John, 96-97, 112-13, 157

Harris, Padre George, 75-76, 92

Hartigan, Sgt. Dan, 68-69, 75, 77-78, 103; and flight over Rhine, 150-51

Hastings and Prince Edward Regiment (Hasty Pees), xi

Hawkins, Jack, 29

Headquarters Company, 1st Canadian Parachute Battalion, 51, 133; D-Day, 106

Hees, Capt. George, 59, 62

Hellerud, Len, 149, 155

Henry, Ed, 37

Hewetson, Col. George: casualties on Rhine drop, 164; Rhine drop, 153, 167-68

Hilborn, Maj. Richard (Dick), 80-81, 133-34, 200; and death of Nicklin, 158; and Dutch people, 137; and Russians, 187

Hill, Brig. James, 16, 72, 77, 200-201; and 1st British Parachute Bat-talion, 46-48; and 1st Canadian Parachute Battalion, 48-49; D-Day, 69, 89-90, 102, 105, 107-10, 112-13; at Merville battery, 90-92; and atrocity at Bande, 131; battle rules, 107-108; in British army, 42-46; and death of Nicklin, 158; early life, 41-43; farewell to Cana-dians, 193-94; and hunger strike, 123-26; new versus old world, 73-74; Rhine drop, 146, 153, 168; run to Baltic, 178, 182; tenets of war, 52-53; wounded in North Africa, 47-48

Hill, Walter Pitts Hendy, 41

Hill Hall transit camp, East Anglia, 145